A Reed
In His Right Hand

Ordinary People Doing Astounding
Things THROUGH GOD'S ANOINTING

EBED
PUBLICATIONS
In love, serve one another

By

Gail Rozell

with Roz Jenkins

A Reed In His Right Hand

Copyright © 1997 by Gail Rozell

ALL RIGHTS RESERVED

EBED Publications is a division of McDougal Publishing, Hagerstown, Maryland

Published by:

ƐBƐƊ Publications
P.O. Box 3595
Hagerstown, MD 21742-3595

ISBN 1-884369-64-2

Printed in the United States of America
For Worldwide Distribution

DEDICATION

This book is dedicated to the first man I ever loved, my dad, to the woman who, by her example, taught me faithfulness, my mom, and to my partner in God's right hand, my husband.

ACKNOWLEDGMENTS

It would be impossible to acknowledge by name everyone who has been involved in this project. Many people have encouraged and supported me along the way, when I might have otherwise given up. A few people, however, deserve special thanks:

Lesley Wheeler and my daughter Cheryl Rozell, for your patient endurance at the computer.

My dearest friend, Lesley, for the title concept.

My daughter Gerrilynn Petersen, Elizabeth Munday, Jeanne Wyns and Kay Bly, for your invaluable suggestions and advice when proofreading. Having an "American Tale" co-written by an English writer proved an interesting challenge, didn't it?

And last, but not least, Roz. You have been a pleasure to work with. You have helped bring a dream to reality, and together we have proven that the Americans and the British can work together after all. Thank you!

My greatest thanks go to the Lord Jesus Christ in whose nail-pierced right hand I forever wish to remain. Unto Him be all the glory!

CONTENTS

About the Title 7

Foreword by Jeanne Wyns 11

Introduction 13

1. The Terrors of Childhood 15
2. Our Damascus Road 20
3. A Higher Calling 26
4. Learning Faith In Zion 31
5. Obedience or Loss 43
6. A Door Opens 50
7. India, At Last! 54
8. It Was Worth It All 60
9. Life In Karachi 67
10. God's Work In Karachi 73
11. Our Love For Children 79
12. People of "One Heart" 84
13. Filling Empty Arms 87
14. Saving the World, and Losing Your Family 96
15. God's Daily Provision For Us 101
16. India Revisited 109
17. Strange Singing In the Night 116
18. Full House – Empty Fields 120
19. Where Is Zimbabwe? 128
20. What's Wrong? 131
21. A Major Career Change 134
22. In Search of the Ostrich People 143

23. A Shy People 153
24. Murder and Its Victims 161
25. The Day Arrives 166
26. Exile And Return 170
27. Enlarge Your Borders 176
28. Mother of Many Nations 178
29. Norbert's Story 181
30. Our Miracle Boy and Others 188
31. Fire and Expansion 193
32. Why Me, Lord? 198

ABOUT THE TITLE

*When they had twisted a crown of thorns, they put it
upon His head, and a reed in His right hand. And
they bowed the knee before Him and mocked him saying, "Hail, King of the Jews."*   Matthew 7:29

Along the banks of the Jordan River in the time
of Jesus the humble reed was everywhere.
No one looked twice at it, for it was an ordinary, insignificant part of the everyday landscape. Then
one day, a reed was thrust into the hand of Jesus as men
mocked Him and placed a crown of thorns on His head.

"Here is the only scepter you're ever likely to hold,
King Jesus, a pathetic stalk of grass." This was the mock-
ing assessment of His tormentors regarding His
sovereignty. But they were wrong. He had a way of taking insignificant things and turning them into something
wonderful and powerful and useful. And He still does.

We must never regard ourselves as too insignificant
to serve God. He is the King of Kings, and in His right
hand the helpless reed is transformed into the mighty
rod of His authority. I know, because He chose me.

The reed is hollow stemmed and, if we are to serve
Him effectively, we must allow the old selfish core of
our lives to be cut away so that God's Spirit can flow
unobstructed through the center of our being. If we sub-
mit to this process, then anything is possible.

The "bruised reed" is mentioned in the book of Isaiah

(42:3), and this passage was quoted by Jesus in the Gospel of Matthew (12:20). What is a "bruised reed"?

One Old Testament word for reed is *ganah* which can also be translated *calamus*. Calamus was one of the ingredients of the sacred anointing oil used to set the priests apart for divine service. Before the fragrance of the oil was released, the ingredients first have to be crushed. Fragrance only arises from the reed that has been bruised or crushed.

There is a bruising aspect of Christian service which I feel is too often covered over, in the fear that men and women will not want to serve Him if they know about it. Serving God *is* about unspeakable joy and victory, but it is also about pain, hurt and severe struggles. There is a strong tendency for Christians to put on a smiling face as a permanent fixture and to hide this bruising aspect of service to God. If we could manage to rip away the exterior, we might often find a drooping mouth of sorrow, pain or doubt.

Why do some ministers run away, abandoning marriages and ministries and everything else they have held dear? Most Christian books that I have read rarely touch on these subjects. They are success orientated, and struggles don't seem to merit much print space with them.

In the pages which follow, I want to talk about the immense joys I have experienced as a missionary, having seen the mighty God at work in spectacular ways. But I also want to deal with my own weaknesses and share with you the stark reality of my failures. Why? Because God brought me through them.

He is not looking for perfect people. Even the familiar Bible characters God used were not perfect. In their

8

darkest moments, however, they all had one thing in common. They knew that they were loved and accepted by a forgiving God.

It is in our struggle that we most need to learn to trust our God and to rely, in faith, upon His strong arms to pull us clear of the downward-sucking swamps of failure. Those who are training for the ministry must expect the sting of pain as well as the buzz of victory, for they will come to know both. The most important key is to know that you are firmly planted in His right hand.

As a young pastor's wife I often felt like a total failure. The more I prayed, the less spiritual I felt. It seemed that nothing I did pleased people. I was lonely and afraid. Even after many years of ministry, I sometimes felt like giving up and escaping through some back door. Yet, God has been faithful to me and has given me fruit for His Kingdom.

What is it that bruises the reed? Often it seems that the people around us or the circumstances of our life are the agents of pain, but the truth is that God Himself allows the bruising to occur so that the sweet fragrance of Christ may be savored.

The reed is deceptively strong. Although it may appear weak, it can endure much. It is quite difficult to break a reed off completely. If there is undue pressure, it may buckle and sometimes sharp snags, which can pierce the skin, will form, but the reed is not easily destroyed.

When the waters of the Jordan flood, it appears that everything has disappeared in the wake of a muddy torrent. But when those waters abate, you can be sure that the reeds will still be there, proudly holding themselves high once again. You and I are just like that.

My prayer and purpose for these pages is that ordinary people may be prepared to hear God's call and abandon themselves wholeheartedly to His service. Although we must be prepared for the bruising that will come our way, we have nothing to fear for God is faithful to His word and will turn every trial into a positive experience in our lives.

I trust that my story will help anyone who reads it to follow confidently the God who has faithfully led me through more than thirty-five years of ministry and will encourage many to become reeds in His right hand, fanning out into all the world with the message of salvation.

FOREWORD BY JEANNE WYNS

(BARNABAS MINISTRIES)

G ail's story will sound familiar to many of you, as it did to me. The feelings of inadequacy that she felt at various junctures of her life are all too common to most of us. As I read the manuscript, it almost seemed that she had stepped into my shoes and lived my life. She has spoken with an honesty and a candor that is refreshing in our superficial world.

She shows us that the difference between the person who becomes a reed in God's right hand and the person who fails is the ability to see the power of God at work in every circumstance of life. It is only His power that can take insignificant people and use them to make a difference in the Earth.

You may be struggling to find a meaningful place of ministry. If so, this book will speak volumes into your spirit about how to allow God full rein so that He can accomplish incredible things in your life. Gail's memories from her childhood will help you to see that God loves you too and that His hand of protection has been upon you for a divine purpose.

Like Gail, you may be a woman battling with the inability to have children. If so, and if you cry into your pillow because your hopes and dreams for the future are dashed again and again, you will be blessed to see how God made Gail a Mother of Many Nations.

If you have ever desired to be a missionary, or to touch some other nation in a significant way, this is the book to be read. Gail's struggle with unfamiliar cultures will amuse, yet challenge you. You will live the drama and enjoy the suspense of the Rozell's initial thrust into a group of totally unreached people in rural Zimbabwe.

You will no doubt weep, as I did, as she recounts several stories of the little ones who are being rescued from death and given new hope for life here and in eternity. As someone who has been to Montgomery Heights Christian Care Centre and seen first hand the loving home, and the tender care that are being provided to these castaway children of Zimbabwe, I rejoice that their story is finally being told. Many of these children were left in garbage heaps or were thrown away because the parents had no money to keep them. The parents of others died of AIDS. I personally witnessed the final few days of Little Leslie on this Earth. An AIDS victim, he spent his final days with loving people who sang with him and prayed with him as he made his final journey from Earth to Heaven.

We are sometimes such poor judges of character. I am sure that Jerry and Gail Rozell and their team will probably never make the front page of our newspapers for their humanitarian acts, but in my books, they are among the greatest people I have ever met, and I count it a privilege to recommend their book. Read it and cry, read it and laugh, read it and allow God to make you "*A Reed In His Right Hand.*"

INTRODUCTION

Somewhere in the world, a mother tries to flush a newborn baby down a toilet because there are already too many mouths to feed in the family. Somewhere in the world a distraught grandmother weeps outside her dilapidated shack; AIDS has just claimed her second child in four months, and she has no food for her grandchildren. Somewhere in the world a teenager hides in the sugar cane fields; she is hungry and afraid; her mother has been murdered, and all her possessions have been burned. Where can she turn for help?

If someone told you that the Great Commission has been fulfilled, think again. In far too many places displaced people with glazed eyes stare into space in the cruel confines of a refugee camp. The intensity of human suffering brought about by wars, famines, disasters, disease and poverty in many parts of the globe is barely imaginable to those of us in the affluent Western nations – despite the images that we regularly see on our evening news.

Vast numbers of people have not yet heard the Good News of Christ's Kingdom and thousands upon thousands of young Christians desperately wait for teaching.

Is all hope lost? Not at all! The heart of the Creator burns with inextinguishable compassion for every human life He has ordained, and He has a strategy for bringing hope and restoration into those broken lives. This strategy involves a massive mobilization of His people, those who are devoted to serve Him in simple faith, who share His love for humanity and who are prepared to sacrifice everything to fight against the darkness that has trapped so many in a pit of despair.

God is looking for men and women who, more than being stirred by noble feelings by an appeal to their emotions, will answer His call and will stick with the task He assigns them when no one is there to see and appreciate their sacrifice.

God is looking for YOU. If you feel that the file of your life so far has "unsuitable" stamped clearly across the front page in red, or you are sure that God could not use someone ordinary like you, maybe it is time to think again. You may well discover that you are exactly the kind of raw material God is looking for. Down through history some of God's mightiest frontline warriors have been the most unlikely characters, regularly dismissed as grossly inadequate by arrogant human committees, but adopted by a God of miracles to do astounding things in His name.

You can be *"A Reed In His Right Hand."*

Gail Rozell
Zimbabwe, Africa

CHAPTER ONE

THE TERRORS OF CHILDHOOD

I woke suddenly, my heart racing so fast that it felt like I had just finished a marathon. Everything was quiet in the house, and I snuggled down into my bed, not realizing at first what had awakened me. Then, a piercing scream, followed immediately by the sound of something smashing, caused me to sit bolt upright.

I was totally awake now, and I could feel my heart sinking like an elevator descending rapidly. *Dad must be drunk again, and fighting with Mom.* Sure enough, more screams and angry shouts followed, and unable to bear it, I pulled a pillow over my head and lay that way for a long time.

Why did they always have to fight? Why did Dad have to drink? I shivered with fright, wondering if he might hurt her badly. *Dad was so soft and gentle when he was not drinking. What happened to him when he was hitting the bottle?*

Hearing a door slam loudly, I got up, and, wrapping the blanket around me, crawled as far as I could into the dark space under the bed. All I wanted to do was escape from the sounds of violence, to pretend that everything was normal in our lives. Yet I knew it wasn't.

Tears ran down my cheeks. *Why did we have to be different from other families?*

Once I had crept downstairs where my father was slumped in a chair sound asleep. I slowly approached him and ever so gently released the bottle from his grasp. Although I felt there was little chance of his rousing, I was still petrified by the thought that he might suddenly wake up and shout at me. But I was able to get the bottle free without waking him, and triumphantly I ran to the kitchen and poured the contents of the bottle down the sink. I felt curiously satisfied as I watched the brown liquid gurgle away. At least we could have a peaceful night that night. *If only every other night were the same.*

Not all of my childhood memories are bad. I remember very vividly, for instance, the day Dad took me on one of his long trips before I was old enough to go to school. He drove a large truck used to haul consignments of potatoes and other goods. This day he was bound for Philadelphia, a trip of a thousand miles or more, and I can still remember the overwhelming excitement and feeling of importance as I was hoisted into the cab that day. What an adventure!

The most wonderful part of the trip came when my father took me into a store to buy me a new dress and some patent leather shoes. They were the first new clothes I had ever possessed, and I felt full of pride and ready to take the world by storm.

But, sadly, what I remember most from my childhood is the loneliness and fear I experienced because I did not feel accepted in my own home, the times I hid in fear from my own father, the embarrassment of unattractive, hand-me-down clothes which caused the children at school to collapse with uncontrollable mirth and made me blush and plot elaborate plans of truancy to avoid the pain of my classmates' derision, and the daily routine of ridicule and cruelty which children are so expert at devising. All in all, growing up was, for me, a traumatic experience

The bottle controlled our family finances and, as a result, our house was full of inferior furniture, and my father drove around the neighborhood in cars that looked as if they should have been consigned to the scrapheap years before. As a sensitive child, I found this to be terribly humiliating.

Our financial situation also meant that we moved around quite frequently, with disastrous results for our early education. The little schoolhouse in Washburn, Maine, where I made my debut into the world of learning, only consisted of two classrooms. My brother and I were in the same class, although he was fourteen months older than me. There I did well in my first year and thoroughly enjoyed my studies. The next year, however, we moved to Connecticut, and the transition from the small rural school to the big city institution proved to be an extremely difficult one.

"Class," I remember my new teacher, Miss Claude, saying that first day, "I want you to copy down the assignment I have put on the board and then complete it." I sat with my pen poised ready to take down the work, eager to prove myself in this new school. But when I looked at the board, I felt very confused. Rubbing my eyes in disbelief, I looked again, but nothing had changed. I stared and stared at the mass of writing before me and began to panic when I realized that I could not read even a single word of it. In Maine, we had been taught to print, but in Connecticut the students our age were already reading and writing cursive. To me, it looked like Greek, and I was hopelessly lost.

"Come on, Gail. Stop staring into space," the teacher said. "Get on with your work." One child snickered at this, and another nearby stifled a giggle.

"What is the problem Gail?"

"Miss ... ," I tried to explain softly and with great embarrassment, "I can't ... I can't read your writing."

"She can't read," a scathing voice declared.

"She's a dummy," another chimed in, and the whole class erupted in laughter.

I desperately tried to hold back the tears that were coming, but my attempts were in vain.

"Look, she's a cry-baby too," someone mocked, and everyone laughed again.

The ordeal of moving from the position of star pupil at our little school in Maine to the dunce of my class in suburban Connecticut was to leave scars on my life for years. I was so far behind these students that I remained an outsider for a long, long time, and I considered the experience one of the more miserable chapters of my life.

The darkest day of my life came, however, when Mother finally decided that she could no longer live with Dad's drunkenness and left him and took us all to our grandparent's house. "Please take Dad back," I pleaded with her. "Give him another chance. Please, Mom." My eyes felt sore from too much crying, and my voice was distorted by sobs.

"Gail, you're too young. You don't understand," she replied wearily as she rocked my newborn sister, Cheryl, in her arms.

"But I miss him," I insisted. "I need him to come back. Please, Mom, for my sake."

The Terrors of Childhood

"Gail, I've already told you it is impossible. I've had enough. Please don't say any more about it. Believe me, we are much better off without him."

Her voice had been sharp and, running from the room, I flung myself on the bed and cried until my pillow was wet with my tears. My heart felt as if it would split apart with pain. Despite his drinking, I still loved my dad very much, and night after night I cried myself to sleep, unable to accept that he had to be separated from us.

It was hard for me to see things from Mom's perspective. Dad's alcoholism had become more than she could bear. Worn down by the endless rounds of assault and verbal abuse, the constant lack of money, and the lies and empty promises, her patience had finally run out. What happened the night Cheryl was born just seemed to be the final straw. Instead of being there to support his wife and family as he should, Dad was out at some local bar. It was soon after this that Mother had asked him to leave, and all my efforts to reunite them seemed to fail.

Then one day things changed. I was looking out the window when I saw a familiar figure approaching. Not needing a second look to identify my father, I hurtled out of the house, threw myself into his arms and clung to him for several minutes. When I finally looked into his face, I saw that he was crying too. Exploding with joy, I danced into the house to tell everyone that Dad was home.

Mother was much less enthusiastic and was, at first, adamant that he must leave. I cried and pleaded with her until she relented and allowed him to stay. I was so happy because we were all together again.

CHAPTER TWO

OUR DAMASCUS ROAD

Dad's return to the home affected us in more ways than one. It didn't take us long to discover that he was a changed man. When Mom had thrown him out of the house, he had returned to our old hometown of Washburn, Maine. Jerked into reality by her decision, he suddenly began to appreciate the family he was losing. He was emotionally devastated by the experience and during the year or so of their separation, he eventually went into a church to cry to God for mercy. This proved to be, for Dad, a Damascus road experience, a life-changing encounter with God.

Just as Saul of Tarsus had been totally transformed by God's power in a single moment of time, so my father's lifestyle radically changed, virtually overnight. He never came home drunk again, and deep compassion and care replaced all the hate and anger he had manifested before. Dad was to become my greatest intercessor. I came to respect him as the Saul who became the Apostle Paul and I wanted, more than anything else in life, to have a similar encounter with God.

Dad was not the only member of our family to influence my spiritual progress. Much earlier, my grandmother had set out to teach me the ways of God. I know that her prayers and example were instrumental in making me what I am in God today. Earliest memories include sitting in the big farmhouse in Maine listening intently to that tiny woman telling me the stories of Jesus. She would often call me her "little missionary." I had no idea what the word meant, but maybe God gave her a glimpse of what He had in store for my life.

Finally, when I was twelve, I gave my heart to Christ. From the start I wanted to be totally dedicated to the task of following Jesus. My desire was to keep my eyes on the goal and stay on course. No diversions for me! I was serious about serving Jesus. When my peers were partying, I was praying. I had been truly born again.

The miracle of new birth is so amazing that many find it hard to accept. Through the years, however, I have known so many people who had similar experiences that I cannot doubt the greatness of what God does through His Spirit. Such a person was Jeff.

I met Jeff in a little storefront church in California frequented by prostitutes, dope addicts and other social outcasts. It was avoided by the popular preachers, but a friend had asked us to go there and preach, and we had gladly accepted the invitation. My encounter with Jeff took place on our second visit to the little church, when I was accompanied by Lesley Marshall, one of our coworkers, because my husband was preaching elsewhere that evening.

I heard a powerful motorbike roar up to the church. When the noise subsided, a large, leather-jacketed biker who looked as if he had been doing overtime in someone's bodybuilding gym strolled inside. Everyone seemed to melt away before him. An arena occupied by Jeff was obviously no place to mount a challenge.

During the entire service Jeff sat on the edge of his seat, and his piercing eyes never left my face. His presence dominated the room, and it was all a bit unnerving for me.

At the end of the service Jeff sauntered up to me with the air of the man who knows his physique guarantees a free passage. "God don't speak to me, lady, like He speaks to you. But He does speak to me," he announced in a deep, gruff voice.

I caught my breath as he proceeded to whisk me off my feet into his huge, dark-stained arms, the skin color obscured by numerous intricate tattoos. When he finally restored me to firm ground he continued.

"I've got a guitar at home, and God told me you'd know someone in Africa who is asking Him for a guitar. God said to me, 'Jeff, you big lunk, you always say you're going to play for Me, but you never do. This lady knows who to give your guitar to, so hand it over.' Will you take it, lady?"

I thanked him and agreed to follow him to his home. Later, we found ourselves roaring across California in hot pursuit of Jeff's enormous motorcycle, praying that his wife would not be hurled to the ground from her precarious perch on the seat behind him. Eventually we arrived at his simple rough wood-framed house, and he presented us with the guitar.

As we were about to leave, Jeff's wife said to him, "Jeff, have you told these ladies how you found Jesus?" Suddenly the unthinkable happened. The confident muscle-man actually seemed to have a serious attack of shyness.

Our Damascus Road

"No. No, they're in a hurry," he said. "They don't have time."

Intrigued, we asked him to tell us his story. What followed has to be the most remarkable testimony I have ever heard:

"I was in the psychiatric unit of San Quentin penitentiary. I had been arrested thirteen times that year, and now I was doing time for slitting someone's throat. There seemed to be no hope for me. I had lost everything; my family and all I possessed were gone. I was going nowhere in life. Then one day a man came and wanted to give me a book.

" 'I don't want your book,' I told him. 'If you want to live, take your book and get out of here.'

"The man laughed and left me alone. Then Jesus Himself appeared to me and said these words: 'Jeff, that book is My Word, and I want you to read it.' I promptly went looking for the man with the book. Finding him, I grabbed him by the shirt, pulled back my fist and said, 'Mister, if you don't want your lights punched out, give me that book.' He willingly obliged.

"Returning to my cell with the book, I prayed, 'Okay, God, You know I can't read, so if You want me to understand the words in this book, You're going to have to do something miraculous.' " Jeff went on to tell us how he then opened the book and read for the first time in his life. This is what he read:

> If we confess our sins, he is faithful and just to forgive us our sins, and to cleanse us from all unrighteousness. 1 John 1:9

"I knew that what I was reading had to be the truth,

because I couldn't read," Jeff continued. "I said to God, 'Okay, God, You know that I am sorry.' And that day God changed my life.

"This place," he continued, pointing to his humble home, "is now known as a halfway house. Since I came to know Jesus, all I have wanted to do is go out under the bridges and to those other places I used to live, and where I used to sin, and tell the people there about Jesus Christ. Then I try to bring them here and help them get on their feet again."

What I heard that day left me speechless. This man had been a desperately violent criminal, someone who was rejected by society because of his savage attacks on other human beings. He had been among the dregs at the bottom of the barrel, and yet Jesus Christ had taken hold of his life and totally transformed him into something beautiful and useful. He would have been one of the first to be thrust into the "unsuitable" pigeonhole by most people without a second thought, but God had given him a new life and a vital role in reaching out to others. Wow!

My own background had absolutely no similarities to that of Jeff, but there is still nothing to mark me out as suitable to be a missionary. I cannot understand even now why God called me to serve Him, but He did. He took my broken life and made something beautiful of it.

My new life in Christ was not to be without struggles, and when I was fifteen the lure of the world destroyed my noble ideals of following Jesus completely. I was soon heading up one of those sidings I had been so determined to avoid. The Enemy is always incensed by displays of devotion to Jesus, and he swung into action with a tactic that has proved highly successful down through the ages in distracting young Christians from God's plan for their lives. I found myself attracted to a non-Christian and began dating him.

Over the next couple of years, gradually, almost imperceptibly God began to slide down my list of priorities. I found more and more reasons why going to church was impossible, and prayer and Bible study were no longer major components of my life. I disdainfully brushed aside my father's warnings, conveniently forgetting that I was not my own and actively pursuing my own selfish ambitions.

There is a very eloquent description of my behavior in the book of Isaiah:

> *All we like sheep have gone astray; we have turned every one to his own way ...*

After two years of that life, however, my bubble was burst. All the excitement had gone out of sin, and rebellion didn't seem such a good idea after all. I thought I loved my boyfriend, and it was hard for me to give him up, but I decided that I loved God more and so I returned to Him in repentance.

CHAPTER THREE

A HIGHER CALLING

Somehow, even from the early years of my Christian experience, I had a strong sense that I had handed over the title deed to my life to Someone who had paid an enormous amount to secure my eternal destiny. I had given up the right to determine my own future, and had voluntarily placed myself in the hands of the Expert Planner of human lives. The Bible puts it this way:

Ye are not your own. For ye are bought with a price.

As a young teenager I had come upon these words in the Bible:

Study to shew thyself approved unto God, a workman that needeth not to be ashamed, rightly dividing the word of truth.

I was absolutely sure that God wanted me to study His Word in a Bible college, and I promised Him that when I had completed high school, I would go on and do that. But, just as living for the Lord daily had proved to be a challenge, following Him into this higher calling for my life was not to be easy either.

A Higher Calling

The poverty in my background had led me very early in life toward a philosophy of working hard to achieve my ambitions through my own efforts. I simply had to become self-reliant. After all, if I didn't take care of myself, who would do it? I was determined to overcome all the obstacles of my childhood and to "make it" on my own.

From as early as I could, I worked and earned my own money. By twelve I was a serious baby-sitter and was buying all my own clothes. I wanted the very best and was determined that the era of secondhand clothes, and of suffering scorn and social rejection because of them, would now be a thing of the past.

At fourteen, I worked all summer in the tobacco fields near my home, toiling from six o'clock in the morning until five o'clock at night. During the school year, I worked in the lunchroom at school to earn free dinners. And by sixteen, I was working a part-time job after school, so that I could be financially independent. My earnings were not all exclusively for myself. We now had a family of nine, and they needed my help too.

An Italian widow gave me a job in her small restaurant that year. Mary was a short, dark-haired lady with a beautiful olive complexion and everyone agreed that she was an excellent cook. It soon became obvious, however, that administration was not her forte. Her late husband had handled that part of the business for her. When it was discovered that I had a flair for the administrative aspects of the business, it was not long before I was doing much more than waiting on tables. I did some of the buying and bill paying and handled other aspects of the business.

One day, after I had been working there for about a

year, I had returned from taking a deposit to the bank, when Mary sat me down in one of the restaurant booths, and we had a long talk. In her pronounced Italian accent she announced, "Gail, I want to ask you something. You have worked very hard since you have been with me. I don't know what I would have done without your help. You are young, but you have proven yourself remarkably astute when it comes to business matters. I would like to offer you a partnership in my business."

My mouth fell open in amazement. *"A partner? In her business?"* I was totally taken aback and did not know what to say. I finally managed to ask, "But what about your children?"

"You don't need to worry about them," she assured me. "None of them are interested in getting involved in the restaurant."

"But I've got no money to invest," I continued. "How could a partnership work?"

"You can work and take from your profits whatever you need to live on. The rest of your share can be used to buy into the business.

"Think about it, Gail. I don't expect an answer here and now. Go home and discuss it with your parents, and let me know what you decide when you can."

I don't remember any details of my walk home that night because my mind was so full that it seemed to be bulging with ideas and possibilities. *What an incredible offer!* I had been working for Mary for about a year, and now to be offered a partnership in her business was heady stuff for a seventeen year old from a poor home. As my imagination was weaving a glorious picture of future success and happiness as a business woman, I was pulled up with a start. What about my promises to God?

A Higher Calling

In my excitement I had allowed myself to forget the conviction that I had deep in my heart that God wanted me to go to Bible college. And suddenly I knew that I was about to face one of the most difficult decisions I had thus far made in life.

Would I accept the opportunity of a lifetime and go into partnership in the restaurant? Or would I obey the call of God to go to Bible college and prepare myself for service to Him? I will have to admit that I struggled with the answer to that question.

Mother was very enthusiastic about the partnership and encouraged me to accept the offer immediately, but I found it difficult to ignore the urgings of the Holy Spirit. He was showing me that a career in the restaurant business was not His perfect plan for my life.

I had made a promise to God, and didn't know how I would live with myself if I failed to keep that promise; still there was a great reluctance on my part to surrender the familiarity of home and my own way of doing things. In the end I made a bargain with God: I promised Him that I would go to Bible college — if I was accepted. I must admit that, secretly, I thought this course was safe. It was late in the year, and I imagined that it was probably too late to be accepted.

My pastor supported me in my belief that God had called me to Bible college and suggested that I write to Zion Bible Institute in East Providence, Rhode Island. I took his advice and applied there.

Then one day I received a letter of response. My hands shook as I opened it. This letter held my future. What would it be?

The letter was very short and sweet and to the point: "We are sorry to inform you that all the places at Zion

Bible Institute for the forthcoming academic year have been filled." I folded the letter, put it back in the envelope and laid it on the table. Then a deep sense of relief flooded my heart. I could go on living my life as I desired.

My conscience would no longer bother me. I had tried to go to Bible college, and I had been rejected. What more could I do? Plans were already forming in my mind concerning my new path in life. I was free.

My freedom was short lived. Hard on the heels of the letter came a telephone call from the principal of the college, Miss Campbell. She told me that one of the students had relinquished her place owing to ill-health and, although the term had actually already started, I was welcome to come and join the class — if I could do so immediately.

Numb with shock, unable to understand exactly what was happening to my world, I suddenly found myself caught up in a whirlwind of preparation to depart and to begin a totally new life. A few days later, with the help of Pastor Sands, I arrived — somewhat disorientated — at Zion to commence my studies with two hundred other students.

CHAPTER FOUR

LEARNING FAITH IN ZION

At first, I felt bewildered and confused by the sharp transition from my old life to this totally new environment. Submerged in a kind of spiritual culture shock, I realized that the grip of the world on my life had been much more tenacious than I had supposed. My general freedom was now left far behind as I struggled to come to terms with a new disciplined regime designed to prepare me to serve God effectively. The process was made somewhat easier by the friends I soon made.

When I first met Pat she was lying stretched out on a top bunk, her dark head resting on her hands as she studied the Bible. She was a petite girl and, when she turned to greet me, I particularly noticed her flashing blue eyes which had an usual arresting quality. She was a third year student, and the friendship that developed between us was an enormous help to me in adjusting to life at Zion.

Pat, a deeply spiritual person, was devoted to prayer. At first her commitment seemed rather strange to me, yet there was a magnetic dimension to her life, and this created a hunger in me to discover the secret of her relationship with God.

"Let's go to the prayer room," she would suggest when I asked her advice about anything at all.

I groaned. *"Why did I bother to ask?"*

Pat invariably found her way to the prayer room whenever the opportunity arose.

"You're altogether too holy for me sometimes," I muttered ungraciously, but I still accompanied her to the prayer room. Her spirituality both fascinated and infuriated me. Sometimes I would find myself boiling with rage at the way she used the Scriptures as her yardstick for everything under discussion. If I disagreed with her, she would challenge me to support my thesis by reference to the Bible — which I was usually unable to do. One side of me resented her ability to get the upper hand in these discussions, while the other side longed for a simple faith like the one she possessed.

Although thirty-five years have now passed since my days at Zion, I can still clearly remember the day she prayed for an ice cream cone. We were out walking one hot afternoon in spring. Absorbed in conversation about some pressing matter, we gradually became more and more uncomfortable in the heat. "Lord, it would be great to have an icecream today," Pat casually mentioned to God.

As neither of us had any money, and since I had some grave doubts about whether petitioning God for ice cream was appropriate, I privately decided that to expect a reply from Him was wishful thinking. We had only walked a few steps, however, when Pat abruptly bent down to pick up something from the path. She straightened and held out her hand which, to my amazement, contained fifty cents. "Thank you Lord," she exulted and, turning to me, she said, "Now, let's go and get an ice cream."

The matter-of-fact way in which she said this suggested that such mundane requests to God were regularly met with a positive response. I was left speechless by the whole affair, but I didn't waste any time in following her into the ice cream shop. Unresolved theological problems were not going to stand in the way of a free ice cream cone.

Faith was not just a hallmark of one student at Zion. For staff and student alike, faith was a lifestyle. What happened one day at lunchtime is a good example.

A great "amen" echoed through the dining hall at the close of the prayer over our meal, and the room filled with the deafening noise of scraping chairs and excited voices, as we all sat down and began to chat. I was dimly aware that the bell was ringing. Gradually silence enveloped the room, as Sister Campbell called for our attention.

"A refrigerated truck has lost its load of food, and that load is currently blocking the road outside the college. The company has agreed to donate the food to the college, but we need your help to move it inside." We quickly evacuated the dining room and began helping to bring in the food items that had fallen from the truck. It took us a while, but it was worth it.

When lunch was finally served, we noticed that some of the same items we had just rescued from the road were on our plates and we wondered about it. Later we discovered the miracle that God had done. When lunchtime arrived there wasn't enough food to serve us. The prayer of thanksgiving that was prayed was not just a formality, it was an act of faith. God had promised that He would supply the needs of His children, and the staff had believed implicitly that He would honor His Word. Their trust was not misplaced. By the time we had all joined in a hearty "amen," a truckload of food had fallen to the road in front of the school and we were soon on our way to retrieve it. This incident had a profound effect on my life.

The whole ethos and teaching of the college revolved around this simple and practical application of faith in God's Word. No one paid tuition fees. If God blessed us financially, we were expected to make a contribution to costs, but we were under no pressure to do so.

Teachers' salaries were by no means a regular stipend. They were encouraged to trust God for their needs, as well, and the men and women who were our teachers at Zion remain my heroes and heroines of faith to this day. Many of them are now with the Lord, but they taught me how to know and trust God. I watched their lives closely and observed that the principles they taught were acted upon in every situation that arose in college life. This teaching on faith has been absolutely vital to the survival of my ministry, and is an indispensable necessity for all who seek to serve God full-time.

In my mind's eye, I can see the heavy-set figure of Sister Rollins pushing back strands of graying hair, and telling us over and over again, "Do not depend upon your mother or father. Do not depend upon your friends. Learn to trust God. When you get out there in the world, at the end of the day it will just be you and God. It does not matter what your friends, family or books have to say. In the last resort, it will be up to you to handle things — with God. In order to do this, you need to have learned to trust Him."

Experience has confirmed repeatedly what Sister Rollins taught us so long ago. I praise God for her and for the other teachers who constantly challenged us when we were so slow to learn to trust God. As I observe the Christian scene today, this kind of total reliance on God seems greatly lacking.

At Zion we were taught that God wants His people to know Him, and that, by definition, a people who know God must be a people of faith. We learned the biblical admonition:

> *But without faith it is impossible to please Him: for he that cometh to God must believe that He is, and that He is a rewarder of them that diligently seek Him.*
> Hebrews 11:6

Because it is obviously not possible for us to see and touch God, we were taught, for He is no longer a tangible part of the world order, our knowledge of Him must arise from faith, and that faith must be anchored in God's Word.

This faith, we were told, is well within the reach of the most ordinary Christians. Belief that God exists indicates a measure of faith which most have and, according to the Bible, removing mountains can be achieved with only mustard-seed-sized faith.

A small amount of faith, we were assured, is highly charged with spiritual power and is capable of completing the tasks God has scheduled for His army. Faith, we were taught, is not something of the past but should be a reality in the present. Faith is for now.

> *NOW faith is the substance of things hoped for the evidence of things not seen.* Hebrews 11:1

Faith is fundamentally active, our teachers showed

us. Running through the streets with a megaphone proclaiming that you have faith does not constitute evidence that faith is an integral part of your life. You have to live it, as the Scriptures declare:

Wherefore by their fruits ye shall know them.
Matthew 7:20

If faith is deeply rooted in our lives, we learned, it will be clearly visible in the way we handle everyday events. Modern technology is all about accelerated living: fast foods, instant advice, quick returns and a total ban on waiting. The world can easily squeeze us into this frenzied mold until our spiritual expectations are affected, and we are looking for fast-acting faith and immediate miracles. The life of faith which my husband and I learned in those years at Zion, and which we have sought to live on a daily basis, has not been easy. We have found that God works in His way, and in His time (which is not always synchronized with ours), but which proves right every time.

Sacrifice and forsaking things which hinder us from obeying God's will are also at the heart of faith. Faith is not a passport to a world of modern convenient, cozy living. Faith is believing God's Word and acting upon it, regardless of the consequences.

As I learned faith, the greatest biblical example seemed to be that of the three Hebrew children. When faced with a "seven times more fiery than normal" furnace, they were able to say these remarkable words:

If it be so, our God whom we serve is able to deliver us from the burning fiery furnace, and He will de-

Learning Faith In Zion

*liver us out of thy hand, O king. But if not, be it known
unto thee, O king that we will not serve thy gods, nor
worship the golden image which thou hast set up.*

Daniel 3:17-18

These men were confident that God had the power to
deliver them, but they did not know for sure if they
would walk free again in this life. They did believe that
God was able to stop them from being incinerated, but
whether or not He chose to do it they could not say. In
any event, their refusal to obey the edict of the king was
not dependent on the promise of an escape route. They
were not prepared to compromise their principles and
worship anything or anyone else but God. Whatever His
immediate plans, He was the only one able to deliver
them, and their allegiance was to Him alone. This was
the faith I wanted to develop.

There were plenty of opportunities to exercise practical faith during my time at college. On one occasion
when I was in my second year, all the students were required to produce one dollar by faith by a particular
Monday morning. After two years in a faith environment
I still had a lot to learn. I eagerly took up the challenge
and was determined to trust God for the dollar.

Faith for one dollar was a good starting point. Building Bible colleges, feeding orphans, running drought
relief projects and all the other major enterprises I have
become involved in since then were not features of stage
one in my faith education program. The Bible makes it
quite clear that it is only after proving ourselves faithful
in small things that our responsibility will be extended
to larger areas.

Nevertheless my lesson in one-dollar faith was a hard

one. I resolved not to write to my mother or ask anyone for help, but I know that I prayed as hard for that dollar as for anything I have ever prayed for. "God, you know that I need this dollar, and if I don't have it by Monday morning both of us will be embarrassed."

By Saturday morning there was no sign of the dollar. I waited impatiently for the mailman, pinning my hopes on a letter containing some money. I was beginning to feel extremely nervous about the whole situation. Rushing to collect my mail, my hopes lifted as I spotted my mother's familiar writing on an envelope. With pounding heart I tore it open; but, alas, even though I turned the envelope inside out, there was no sign of the dollar I needed. Things were beginning to look very serious — and my prayer, as well: "Lord, time is running out fast. PLEASE will You provide this dollar."

I cheered up slightly when I remembered that some young people from my home church were coming to visit me that evening. On previous occasions someone had usually been moved to slip five dollars into my hand before leaving. But this time, my friends came and my friends departed, and even though I feverishly checked every corner of my room for concealed anonymous gifts in unlikely places, there was nothing to be found.

Serious doubts now began to rise in my mind. Virtually every channel by which I could expect to receive a dollar was closing, and time was running out. There would be no more mail and no more visits from friends until after the deadline for handing over the required dollar.

"God, You're not going to let me down, are You?" I prayed earnestly. "I trust You, but aren't You cutting this thing a bit close?"

Learning Faith In Zion

The suspense was terrible, and when I considered how embarrassed I would be when the moment came and I had no money, I could have kicked myself for not simply asking my mother for it. Now there wasn't time even for that.

On Sunday morning I sat in church with my mind far removed from the service, as if I had been resident on another planet. Having a dollar in my possession on Monday morning preoccupied my thinking. As I came out of church I noticed an old lady waiting to cross the road. She was one of a group of retired teachers who had remained at Zion after their teaching years came to an end. Those who had no family were cared for by the college. I managed to detach myself sufficiently from my selfish concerns to help the lady across the road and, as we stood chatting, an elder from the church joined us. He invited the elderly teacher to go for a ride in the afternoon, and I ended up joining the party with my first-year roommate.

I must have been terrifically stimulating company that afternoon, constantly losing the thread of conversations because my mind was still wrestling with the problems of the missing dollar. This was not the best way to endear myself to others. Even as we traveled through the countryside, my prayer intensified. "God, it is the eleventh hour. Where is my dollar? Have You forsaken me, Lord?" I silently cried out in desperation.

We stopped at an ice cream parlor. The elder and the older lady sat in a booth talking, while my friend and I perched on high stools at the counter. Once again I drifted off into fantasies which featured the miraculous discovery of dollar bills at the bottom of the ice cream glass, and so I did not notice the church elder come up behind us. The sound of his voice startled me.

"I know this isn't much, but maybe you need a tube of toothpaste or something," he said as he handed each of us a dollar. I could not believe what was happening and was so excited that I nearly lost my balance and fell off the stool. If it had been a million dollars, I could not have been more thrilled. Even though my faith had wobbled dangerously, I had trusted God to supply that dollar, and He had been faithful to me. I had to learn that God often supplies our needs in ways which we could never have anticipated, and often at the last minute.

Whenever I have needed thousands of dollars in subsequent years, I have reminded myself of those days when God faithfully supplied one dollar in the nick of time. That experience has never failed to encourage me to trust Him for larger sums.

I was talking to a friend recently who was at Zion with me. She too was a missionary in Zimbabwe and now has a worldwide ministry. She agreed that without the faith foundation we received at college, we would have failed to see visions through to their fulfillment and would have floundered in many other ways in our years of Christian endeavor. I long for other Christian colleges to be established that can bequeath to their students the legacy of faith that was given to us at Zion.

Zion Bible Institute also placed great importance on having an accurate grasp of the Word of God. The final test in my personal evangelism course required us to know one hundred scripture verses. In some cases the scripture had to be quoted, and in others the reference given. When my paper was returned, I had scored ninety-nine percent. The quotation marked wrong was John 3:16. It seemed ironic that I had made a mistake on the most well-known verse in the whole Bible. I read and reread what I had written and could not see an error. So, I went back to the teacher to complain.

"You marked this wrong," I told the teacher, "but I cannot find any mistake."

"Gail, the Bible says, *'whosoever believeth in Him,'* but you have written 'whosoever believeth on Him,' " she replied.

"But surely it means exactly the same thing," I responded defensively.

"It is vital, if you expect to teach the Word of God, that you know it thoroughly," she told me. "The misquotation of Scripture, however slight, is the route to the formation of cults and sects."

At the time her response seemed to me to be a gross overreaction to a very minor mistake, but now I can appreciate the importance of this seemingly rigid approach. Throughout my ministry I have continued to be very conscious of the need for one hundred percent accuracy in the use of the Scriptures.

Another of the lessons I learned during my college days which later became a solid building block on which my ministry would be built came through our friendship with a nun. One day she described the Christian life as a ball game. Some people are out on the field engaged in the exhausting battle for supremacy, while others watch indolently from the stands. Her desire was always to be an active player on the field and not a spectator confined to the stands.

I adopted this philosophy as my own. Action on the field, seeing men's and women's lives changed by God's power, however great the personal sacrifice, became the desire of my heart. I am convinced that God is searching for people today who are prepared to come down from the relative comfort of the stands and take their place on the field of action for Him.

Gradually my time at Zion, and all I was learning regarding dynamic faith, charged my life with new meaning. Hours spent in the prayer room with Pat deepened my awareness of God's voice. On one occasion, as we were praying, I saw a vision of myself preaching from the book of Isaiah to an enormous crowd of brown-skinned people who spoke an unfamiliar language. I knew that this vision was significant, but it was to be several years before I understood and realized its full impact.

Returning to college for my second year had been difficult. Pat had graduated, and I missed her encouragement and companionship. I still visited the prayer room often, that place where we had spent so many hours together seeking God and pouring our hearts out to Him, and every time I did I prayed for Pat. One day my prayer was something like this: "Lord, if Pat is ever in a place of desperation, let me be Your hand extended to her."

Ten years later, when we had lost contact completely, God reminded me of that prayer. "This is the day," He seemed to whisper, and I sensed that my friend was in some serious trouble. I didn't know where she was living, so I contacted her mother and learned that she was living in California — more than three thousand miles away. I wrote Pat a letter. I later learned that when my letter came, Pat had been close to death and had no one to help her. The Lord made it possible for me to go and help her.

CHAPTER FIVE

OBEDIENCE OR LOSS

During that second year of Bible college, a new friendship began to develop. Jerry Rozell was in the third year, but somehow we had not particularly noticed each other until then. As we began to talk and spend time together, a bond quickly grew between us. We were not permitted to formally date at college, but Jerry and I seized every opportunity to talk after church and after class or around the campus wherever we would see each other. We both wanted to serve God wholeheartedly and knew therefore how vital it was to marry the person of God's choice. Jerry proposed to me one day, while nonchalantly leaning against a fence. His proposal had a very strong condition attached to it.

"I have to tell you, Gail, that I want to marry you, but I know that God has called me to India. If you marry me, then you must be willing to go too."

I wasn't offended by this strange proposal, and as Jerry spoke, the brown faces I had seen in the prayer room suddenly seemed to pass before my eyes, and I understood what God was saying. "God has already spoken to me about going to India," I quietly responded.

We were blessed to have similar callings. Happiness

in marriage is never an easy thing to achieve. There are so many potentially divisive factors, any one of which can alienate a spouse's affections. When two people marry, and only one of them has a call of God to ministry, the stage is set for a tempestuous drama.

For young people and people of all ages who are feeling the emotions of love, it seems so easy to silence the voice of warning on this issue and to convince yourself that everything will turn out well in the end. Many marriages and many ministries have been wrecked on this particular rocky reef.

Ministry itself is far from being a trouble-free zone, but somehow, if both partners share one heart to serve God in the way He has called them, they are then able to pull together in the storms.

We were not alike in every other way. Jerry was an only child, while I came from a family of seven. This was just one of many differences in background and ideas that we brought to our marriage, but we had one heart to serve God, and His love in us has enabled us to triumph.

Soon after we left Bible college, Jerry and I married and began to make plans to go to India. It was 1962.

Once our commitment to each other had been affirmed, we were both eager to get to the field and get on with the job God had called us to do there. Jerry was quite unprepared for the response he received when he was interviewed by the head of the Missions Department of the denomination to which we belonged.

"India. Out of the question I am afraid. The Indian government does not allow Christian missionaries to work in the country. It is impossible to go there."

Jerry protested, "You say that it is impossible to get

into India, but God has told us that He wants us to go there. Surely He wouldn't tell us to go if there is no way to go."

"No, I am afraid not," came the answer from the senior missionary. "Maybe God wants you to go sometime, but He obviously does not intend you to go at this point in time. I assure you that no one is going to India at the moment."

After we had discussed it at length, we decided that such experienced missionaries must know what they were talking about. Perhaps God had just been trying to establish that we were *willing* to go to India. We had not yet learned that if God is prompting you to do something, it will happen, even if an army of experts tell you that it is impossible. I was still only nineteen, and we had a lot to learn.

In some ways, the verdict of the head of the Missions Department was a relief. After the first flush of excitement at being called to mission work in such an exotic place like India, I had begun to wonder what life would be like there. I wanted to do God's will and go where He directed, but if that was not to be India, so much the better.

During holidays from school, I had continued to work in the restaurant where I had been offered the partnership, and now my Italian friend invited me back on a full-time basis. And why not? We had done what God had said in completing Bible college, then when we tried to apply for service in India, the door had shut. Why not get back to learning the art of being a business woman. I felt like I had every right to settle back into a "normal" life.

Jerry and I rented an apartment, bought some beautiful furniture and, without realizing it, began to find materialistic values creeping into an increasingly central position in our lives. Jerry was not as relaxed about this as I felt I was. Sometimes he would come home from work, sink into a comfortable chair, and say to me, "Gail, I'm sure that God wants us on the mission field. What should we do about it?"

"No, I don't think it is necessary," I would reply.

"But if God is speaking, don't you think we should at least try to find out what we can do?"

"Jerry, we have been through all this before," I answered. "We've been told that we cannot go to India, so I don't want to think about it any more. I just want to get on with my life. Is that too much to ask?"

So the subject was dropped — for the moment.

One Valentine's Day evening we wearily turned into our drive after a hectic day at work. Jerry flipped open the mailbox, extracted a few letters, and we went in the house. I kicked off my shoes and collapsed into the softness of a living room chair. Sitting across from me, Jerry slit open an official-looking envelope, removed the letter inside, and got ready to read it.

"Well, at least I know it can't be from a secret admirer, in an envelope like that," I joked. "What is it?"

He didn't reply, but just stared blankly at the page.

"What's the matter Jerry? What's wrong?"

"It's the Army. I'm about to be drafted. I've got to go for a physical first."

"Drafted! You can't be. Jerry, we just got married. They can't make you leave me now!" I began to weep. I just couldn't face the thought of being separated from him. "You can't go, Jerry. I won't let you go!" I cried angrily.

Looking pale with shock himself, Jerry tried to comfort me. *What a terrible thing to happen to us on Valentine's Day!* we both thought.

In the days that followed I tried to reason with God. "Lord, it's just not fair. We're Christians. We're trying to live the way You want us to live. You can't let this happen to us." But nothing seemed to be happening.

The day for the physical came, and Jerry went to catch the train to Fort Dix, New Jersey. While he was away, I prayed like I had never prayed before, pleading with God not to take my husband away from me in this way.

During Jerry's absence God began to deal with me. He spoke very clearly to me, saying, "You have not been willing to do what I wanted you to do, and therefore you now have to make a choice. Either you choose to go My way, or I am going to take him into the Army. He has become too important in your life. He is more important to you than I am."

I'm not sure I understood all that God was saying at the time, but I have since come to understand that while it is not wrong to have a husband whom you love very much and it is not wrong to be devoted to your children, it *is* wrong to give them a more important position in your life than you give God.

I was broken by what God told me that day, and I began to cry out to Him, admitting that He was right and vowing to change my ways. "God, if You will only bring him back safely to me," I prayed, "I will do whatever You say. I will go wherever You want me to go. Please, hear me, Lord. Please hear me."

When Jerry returned home the next day, however, the news was not good. He had passed the physical and had been sent home to make preparations for leaving for boot camp. He would soon have to begin his required stint in the Army.

I could hardly believe what I was hearing. There was no way out now. We were in the clutches of the U.S. Army, and that was the end of the matter. I was devastated.

Having felt sick for several days, I decided to consult my doctor. It seemed I must have caught a virus that was currently doing the rounds. The doctor asked a few questions and then smiled. "Well, Mrs. Rozell, there is a very simple explanation for your sickness. You're expecting a baby. Congratulations!"

Somewhat dazed, I left the doctor's office and made my way home. It was only on my way home that the full implications of this pregnancy suddenly dawned on me. If a man's wife was expecting, that was grounds for being dismissed from the draft. Jerry would not have to leave me after all. I was sure of it.

"Oh thank You, Lord. Thank You," I cried and sped home to tell my husband the amazing news.

To my utter relief, Jerry *was* allowed to remain at home, and I was full of excitement at the prospect of becoming a mother. I had always wanted a family of my own, had always loved children and, being the oldest girl in a family of seven, I had been initiated early into the realities of raising them. When I was just seventeen someone had given me a prophecy saying that I would be the mother of many. The actual words of the prophecy were "mother of many nations," but all that registered with me at the time was the fact that I was to have many children. I was, therefore, crushed when Mother's Day found me lying in a hospital bed, utterly desolate, having lost our first child.

Obedience or Loss

I would like to be able to say that I turned to God in my distress and received from Him the grace and comfort I needed. The fact is that I was consumed with anger. I was angry with people, and I was angry with God. This baby was supposed to be the beginning of my family, the family *He* had promised. I had been so looking forward to becoming a mother. Now my heart was full of bitterness and angry questions. *How could God have allowed this tragedy to happen to me?*

I remember waking up and discovering that someone had left some flowers by my bed. "Where did these flowers come from?" I asked a neighbor.

"Oh, someone from a church came in and distributed them to all the mothers for Mother's Day," I was told.

"Well, I'm not a mother," I cried, "and I don't want any flowers." A torrent of rage welled up inside my heart as I picked up the offending flowers and hurled them across the ward.

As I look back over this period in my life, I know that I could have saved myself a lot of anguish and heartache if I had only been prepared to obey God and not insist on getting my own way. My stubborn heart had pursued what I wanted in life and not God's perfect will for me, and I had to pay a price for that.

CHAPTER SIX

A DOOR OPENS

Jerry and I sat in the darkened hall watching dusty streets, Hindu temples and brown faces flickered across the screen. A visiting minister, the Rev. B.G. Drake, who knew absolutely nothing about us, was showing slides of India at our church. As scenes of terrible deprivation and distress passed in front of our eyes, I felt something wrenching at my heart. I remembered all that God had said to us regarding India, and the tears began to fall. Jerry was weeping too.

By the time the lights were switched on, we had regained our composure, and not a trace of a tear could be detected. As the lights came on, the minister began to walk down the aisle toward the pew where we were sitting; he stopped, looked at us and spoke these words, "Has God ever spoken to you about going to India? He has just told me that when I go back I must take you with me. Can we talk?"

Somewhat dumbfounded we agreed, and later that evening we met with the Rev. B. G. Drake and our pastor and his wife, Brother and Sister Sand, in a small restaurant. They knew of our call to India and was prepared to give us their support.

A Door Opens

"Do you want to go to India with me?" he asked.

The only way I could cope with the emotion of the moment was to answer lightheartedly, " Why not? If God can pay all my bills and provide a ticket then I'll come."

The minister looked at me with a very serious expression in his eyes and replied, "I am not joking. I believe that God wants you to go."

The smile quickly faded from my face, and I felt rather foolish. Our pastor was convinced that God had opened up this way for us to go to India after all the negative responses we had received to our previous inquiries. After much prayer and discussion, we finally decided that India was indeed the destination God had in mind.

There remained many obstacles for us to overcome before we were free to leave the United States. For one thing, we had managed to get ourselves quite heavily in debt. It is so important for us as Christians that we do not create financial prisons for ourselves. Then we find our movements are restricted when God wants us to move on. Apart from this, obviously debt is not a very good position for a child of God to be in.

We sold many things, and in a couple of months were able to clear all our debts. God also provided us with enough money to buy our airline tickets.

Financial problems were not the only source of anxiety at this time. The old twinges of hesitation I had experienced at the thought of actually living in the Far East reappeared, only this time they were a searing pain of fear. Victory over my fears was elusive, to say the least. I was just twenty and had never lived that far from home. Although there had been many troubles in my childhood I was deeply attached to my parents, and the thought of leaving them was unbearable.

As we prepared to go away, sometimes my heart would leap with excitement at the prospect of going to India, but on other days I could not face thinking about living in a land of strange new customs far away from my family. My feelings were caught up in a kind of emotional tennis match. As time began to run out, I was gripped by a sense of desperation. One day I walked into a bedroom at home where my baby sister Lori was lying in her crib. I picked her up in my arms, and tears of sorrow ran down my cheeks.

"God, I don't know when I'll see her again, and even if I do, she will be grown up, and we won't even know each other. I can't bear it, God."

The Enemy was active in sowing seeds of doubt in my mind. I became convinced that if I went to India, I would never see my mother and father again, and the thought of leaving them behind was tearing me apart inside.

Just days before our departure, I suddenly announced to Jerry, "Well, you can go to India, and I hope you enjoy yourself, but I'm not coming."

He looked at me, his face registering considerable alarm. "What do you mean, Gail?" he asked in desperation.

"What I said. I'm not going. I changed my mind. I don't want to go to India."

A war was going on in my life. My flesh had launched a vicious offensive against my spirit. I knew deep down in my heart that God wanted me to go to India, and my spirit was willing to obey, but my flesh had other ideas. It was a tough fight. At the end of the day, I knew that I had to be prepared to lay down my life. I had to be able to say to God that, even if it involved never seeing my parents again, my choice would be to follow Him. I had the Lord's assurance:

> *And everyone that hath forsaken houses, or brethren, or sisters, or father, or mother, or wife, or children, or lands, for my name's sake, shall receive an hundredfold, and shall inherit everlasting life.*

This makes stirring reading when God is actually calling you to literally put it into practice. The stark truth was that every fiber of my being was shrieking, "I want to stay at home."

I did agree to go in the end, but I did not leave American soil walking tall in confident faith as befits a missionary of any substance. Everyone came to Bradley Airport to wish us well and pray for us, but all I did was cry into a succession of soggy tissues. Hours later, when the plane touched down in Paris, I was still weeping, and looked most unattractive, with swollen red-rimmed eyes.

During a tear-free interlude, I began talking to a small boy. "Where are you going?" he asked me.

"I'm going to India," I replied, feeling as if I was about to choke.

The boy explained that his father was the pilot of the plane and, as he talked about his father, I became engulfed in a terrible loneliness and turned away from him. Convinced that I would never see Dad again, I began to sob. It was in fact all a lie. I saw my father many times after that, but the memory of the pain and suffering of that journey, as I allowed my imagination to conjure up a succession of ever more alarming consequences of the trip to India, would probably never be erased from my mind.

CHAPTER SEVEN

INDIA, AT LAST!

S uddenly we were plunged into a land of new experiences, sights, sounds and smells. Sometimes we were overwhelmed with the sheer joy of seeing God at work in incredible ways. At other times we felt bewildered, lost and lonely as we tried to cope with super-hot curries, filthy, insect-ridden accommodations, frustrating language barriers and all other manner of cultural problems in the ever-changing scenery of the many towns and villages we visited.

We also had to keep a sharp eye on our finances, as we had left America with only six hundred dollars and a one-way ticket. Some would probably have accused us of foolishness in that regard, but we were trusting God to see us through.

The whole subject of food became a major issue for me in India. I was a fastidious eater, and all the spicy Indian meals were an anathema to me. One day God had to take me in hand.

We were visiting an orphanage which was housed in a primitive dirt-floored building. It was lunchtime, and a sea of brown faces greeted us. Each child was holding a tin plate, waiting for a helping of the inevitable rice and curry. One little boy came up to me, having collected his food, and shyly offered me his plate. I was in a terrible quandary. The look of the food repulsed me, and I had no desire to eat it, but how could I refuse this winsome child who was smiling up at me and offering to share with me? He would never understand. I smiled bravely and took the plate.

"Where do you suppose the cutlery is?" I asked the others.

"It's right here," I was told as a member of our group held up his fingers, grinning broadly. The whole situation assumed new proportions of horror as I realized I was expected to use my fingers instead of knives and forks. God touched my heart that day through a child who had nothing and yet was prepared to share his lunch with me. I began eating the curry with my fingers from the tin plate. And that day I began my liberation from cultural bondage.

The conditions in the places we stayed contributed considerably to this process of liberation from our highly sanitized lifestyle. One night, totally exhausted after hours of travel, we ended up at the Alpha Hotel. Believe me it was the Alpha and the Omega. Our host had neglected to make reservations for us, and, at this late hour, everything else was filled. To register, we were forced to pass through a dingy bar where the clientele, in various stages of inebriation, sagged over tables or leered at us from their high stools. We didn't like the looks of things, but it was either stay in the Alpha or sleep in the street. Not much of a choice!

As we went upstairs to our room, I tried not to think of all the women of ill-repute who had doubtless climbed the same narrow winding staircase. The dingy walls were splattered with sinister red stains, giving one the impression that some poor victim's blood had flowed down their grime encrusted surface. Later we would learn that it was, in reality, the spit from those who chewed beetlenut. I shivered at the sight.

When we opened the door to our room, we were met with the smell of urine coming from a filthy toilet situated in one corner. The place seemed to shriek: "Serious disease zone! Approach at your own risk!"

I had visions of the rows and rows of toilet cleanser and enormous cans of disinfectant on sale in the supermarkets back home, and at that moment would have given anything to lay my hands on a few of them. We tried not to betray our feelings to our hosts, but it was extremely difficult, especially when I realized that the walls were thick with a veritable colony of cockroaches lying head to tail in an idyll of intimacy. I choked back a scream and turned my attention to the tiny steel-framed bed and what looked like a doubled-over blanket which apparently was the mattress. Pillows, sheets or other bed coverings were nowhere to be found, which, in the circumstances, was probably just as well.

We had only a few minutes to recover before it was time to leave again to get to a local meeting where we were scheduled to minister. It felt to me as if a lifetime would not be sufficient to recover from the thought of actually spending a night in this filthy hole. The heat was suffocating; a car horn blared, drowning for a moment the other night noises that arose from the busy streets below, and all I wanted to do was cry. I sank down on to the hard bed.

"Oh Jerry, what are we going to do? This place is horrible. I can't stand it," I wailed.

The stoic missionary of our ideals, that person who had self so firmly under control that he welcomed adversity with open arms and counted it a privilege to lie down in a squalid hole immediately able to see it transformed into a corner of Heaven by the presence of Christ, had little in common with my feelings at that moment.

Jerry tried to comfort me. "It's okay. Gail. We'll make it. One step at a time. We need to get ready for the meeting right now."

As I sat in the service that night I could not blot out the picture of that terrible room. I dreaded going back to it and began to hope that the meeting might go on forever.

Later, as I tossed and turned in that smelly, insect-infested room, I wrestled with the problem of why God would allow this to happen to me. *Surely I deserve better than this*, I reasoned.

Modern teachers of prosperity often seem to suggest that walking with God is one long stay in a luxury hotel. Well, all I can say is that God didn't take us down that road. He took care of our needs, and He gave us miracles, but it was not always in a luxurious environment.

Later that night I woke up feeling chilled. "I'm so cold. So very, very cold," I told Jerry with chattering teeth. My body was shivering uncontrollably, even though I am sure the temperature had not fallen all that much. I was able to get up the next morning, but I didn't feel well at all. Noticing that my body was covered with red blotches, I concluded that I must have contracted something like measles.

We had not had a decent meal in days, so the team we were working with decided to take us to another hotel where good food was served. One of the group, noticing that I was not well, asked me, "What is the trouble, Gail?"

"I'm not sure," I answered. "I'm covered with these

red spots. Do you think I have measles?" I pointed to a few of the spots that were visible.

"Those are bed bug bites," the man answered, "and it looks to me as if you might have malaria."

This was the sort of news I could have done without. I hardly knew what a bed bug was. They had not been a regular feature of life in the United States. As for malaria, that sounded serious. By this time, however, I didn't feel much like learning more about either one. All I wanted to do was go back to the room and lie down. I felt so bad that I forgot the cockroaches and the bed bugs.

My fever raged for the rest of that day, and I was barely conscious of what was going on around me. Dimly aware of the arrival of the ministry team, I assumed it must be time for them to move on to the next meeting. Jerry must have told them he could not leave me in this semi-delirious state, and I was vaguely aware that they prayed for me. Soon after they left, the fever abated, and I began to recover. God had reached down into that run-down hotel and healed me. In the days that followed all that remained of my sickness were some fever blisters in and around my mouth.

We soon moved out of the hotel, as everyone had agreed that it was not wise for us to remain there any longer, and a lovely Indian family took us in and tried to make us feel at home. It was a vast improvement on the infamous Alpha Hotel, but with chickens trying to improve their sprinting techniques under the kitchen table, it was a little difficult to imagine that we were in family surroundings.

By now Christmas was approaching, and our thoughts inevitably kept straying to our families back in America. The Indian family went out to uproot a tree, in the hope that a substitute Christmas tree would be therapeutic for our spirits. Their tree bore no resemblance whatsoever to a traditional Christmas tree, but we were deeply touched by their efforts to ease our homesickness.

The eighteen months that we spent travelling in India and West Pakistan turned out to be an all-out assault on us — physically, emotionally and spiritually. Hour after hour we would travel to meetings in disintegrating vehicles that would have long since been consigned to the scrap heap back home. Some were minus floor boards, and the dust would fly up inside the vehicle smothering us in a layer of gritty sand and dirt. Sometimes we would arrive at meetings in an extremely dishevelled state, looking as if we had been rolling around in the dust for hours. We would preach and pray for the sick and repeat the car journey in the opposite direction, falling into bed at the end of the day, often in a health-hazard of a room.

Week after week this went on, until we felt totally exhausted. Sometimes I would cry myself to sleep yearning for familiar things around me and for someone familiar to whom we could talk. Ministry can be very lonely sometimes.

People see the public image of a man or woman anointed by God and can sometimes be deceived. There is a life beyond the platform, and sometimes that life reflects great cost. When the anointing of God is upon you, you feel as if you can take on the world singlehanded. When the crowds have gone home, however, and you climb aboard some old boneshaker and find yourself choking on the dust coming up through the floor, it is a very different story. Only God's Word keeps you.

Chapter Eight

It Was Worth It All

There was a flipside to our experiences in India which made it all worthwhile. Having told the negative side, I must add that I would not have missed those days for anything in the world. There was an enormous sense of excitement as we saw God working miracles that we had never seen before, and we were conscious of His presence with us and His faithfulness to us in new ways, despite all our shortcomings. We were happy to be part of His powerful invasion of this part of the world.

On one occasion I accompanied an Indian pastor out to a very remote area to preach. At the end of the meeting one of those who came forward for prayer was a little ten-year-old girl. She had been born deaf. I laid my hands upon her and prayed that God would enable her to hear.

I looked into her face to see if there was any reaction and soon realized that the child was absolutely terrified. She covered her ears with her hands and bent her head to the ground. For the first time in her life she was hearing and what she heard was the sound of thousands of people singing and praising God. Her silent world had been split open and the sudden volume was too much for her to comprehend.

To see that girl hear for the first time after a simple

prayer of faith was an unforgettable experience and an immense privilege. I had read the stories of miraculous healings in the Bible so many times and I had heard numerous modern testimonies, but this was the first time I had seen God do something spectacular with my own eyes. I was speechless with wonder. Encountering the power of God in this way changed my life.

On another occasion I was in an open-air meeting where two to three thousand people were present. So many people wanted our prayers that we had to divide them into four prayer lines so that each of us could minister to as many as possible.

Sometimes we ministers leave our Bible schools with the shelves of our minds well stocked with theories that make us seem to be experts. There is nothing like a strong dose of the real world to make us appreciate and experience our own limitations. In the real world, overinflated egos get deflated in a hurry.

In my particular prayer line that day I was faced with a girl of about twenty who was a deaf-mute. Her friend who had brought her to the meeting told me that she had been that way from birth. Inwardly I gulped, crying out to God for help. Just as I laid my hands on her, I heard a strange noise behind me. Wheeling around, I saw a demented-looking girl charging in my direction growling like a wild animal. I froze in panic. I felt like I should run for my life, but my feet seemed to be glued to the ground. In one moment, all my theories about demon possession were carried away like leaves in a stiff breeze, and I had no idea what to do next.

When the demented girl was almost upon me, the Holy Spirit spoke into my heart: "Greater is He that is within you. You have greater power. You have the authority." I firmly rebuked the spirit in the name of Jesus and, much to my relief, the girl veered away from me and tore off across the fields.

Feeling extremely weak in the knees from that strange experience, I turned back to the deaf-mute girl and laid hands on her again, and she was instantly healed of her deafness. Oddly enough, although the girl could now hear and make sounds, she had difficulty forming actual words. Although I was young, God gave me wisdom at that moment, and I realized that she would have to learn to speak, as all of us do. I told her friend to start working with her and teaching her to speak. Sure enough, when she came back the next day, she could already stutter, "Praise the Lord," and within a few days she was able to say many words in a perfectly normal way.

This girl had not come from a poor family. One of her sisters was studying medicine in the States. But, because of her condition, which many attributed to demons, she had been an outcast. Now God had done a great miracle in her life and everyone who knew her was amazed.

God's power was displayed in many other types of miracles during those days. One day we sought permission from local officials to preach in an area administered by a communist government. "You cannot preach the Gospel here," we were told, and that seemed to be final. But God had another way for us to gain access to the people.

I was invited to visit a local girls' school to speak about our American system of education. As my knowledge of American education was sketchy, to say the least, I was not very enthusiastic about this prospect. I was even less enthusiastic when I was told, in no uncertain terms,

It Was Worth It All

that I must not mention the Gospel in my talk and that I must visit the school alone, unaccompanied by my companions.

That sounded rather ominous to me, and I had visions of a lonely country road, the sound of gunfire and a shallow grave containing my body. I should have been more spiritual and trusted God but, frankly, I was terrified. In the end the school officials relented and allowed Jerry to accompany me, on the condition that he would remain silent.

We rode to the school in one of those vehicles with no floor to speak of. After going through the all-too-familiar de-dusting routine, we were ushered into a hall and took our place at a long table lined with men dressed in traditional Indian costume. They looked very smart in their long, gleaming white shirts worn over colorful baggy trousers, but their faces were set in grim unwelcoming expressions and, by the time I finally was called on to speak, my knees felt decidedly wobbly.

Hundreds of young Indian girls, each dressed in a beautiful sari, stood silently facing me, waiting for the lecture on American education. Deciding that honesty was definitely the best policy, I admitted up front that I was far from being an expert on the subject we were about to consider, but that I did know a little more about Christian education in our country. In the moments that followed, somehow the Lord helped me to use the situation to tell those young girls something of the impact God had made on my life personally. As this unfolded, I tried not to think of the grim brigade of communist officials at the table, who remained inscrutably silent for the duration of my talk.

My words were very well received, and, as a result of

this visit, many other schools opened their doors to us and we were able, in this way, to declare the Gospel in this formerly "closed" area.

Before it was over, our men were invited to preach in the schools, and we were even offered full-time positions to teach the Word of God as a regular subject. What had begun as a delicate situation had turned into a glorious outreach for the Gospel to the surrounding areas.

Another strange place we preached was in the "Graveyard Church" in Madras. An uneasy feeling hovered somewhere in the pit of my stomach as we neared the dark and eerie atmosphere around the derelict cemetery on the outskirts of the city. Long grass brushed against my legs as wooden crosses, in various stages of disrepair, loomed out of the shadows. I tried very hard to concentrate on the task in hand. This would not be the most comfortable place to preach.

When we were ready to pray for the people, many demon-possessed people came forward. In such sinister surroundings, it was easy to imagine that they might be people who had come up out of the nearby graves, and I had a strong desire to turn and run. But God was faithful to us once again, and many people were delivered, healed and brought into a living relationship with God through Jesus Christ.

Our original team had split up and gone separate ways, in order to be able to respond to the many invitations we had to minister. When B.G. came to Madras, we met in a local hotel. While we were telling him what a wonderful time we were having in India, he asked, "How did India become so significant for you?"

"It was at Bible college," Jerry replied. "We were

watching a movie, *The Cry of India*, when God told me that I would one day preach in India."

"Did you say *The Cry of India*?" he asked.

"Yes, that's right," Jerry said. "Have you seen it?"

B.G. was visibly moved, and there was a pause before he could answer: "Yes, I've seen it," he said. "I've seen it many times. In fact I made it."

We could hardly believe what we were hearing. His simple film had been widely circulated in the States and had somehow come to our Bible college. God had used it to touch Jerry's heart and then had later sent the moviemaker himself to the very church we were attending to single us out to accompany him to India. What a mighty God we serve!

It has always been breathtaking to us to be given a glimpse of the incredible masterplan of God in bringing people together to help build His Kingdom, and that day in Madras was no exception. Awe and wonder were just two of the many emotions we experienced in those moments.

We continued to preach in the Madras area. One day I was preaching from the book of Isaiah and suddenly had a strong sense that I had experienced before what was happening at that moment. At first, I couldn't understand what I was feeling, but then I remembered the vision I had received in the prayer room at Zion. A vast crowd of brown-skinned people had been listening to me preach from the book of Isaiah, and here they were in reality before me. Many of those present came to Christ that day, and I was so thrilled to see not only how God was working for us in the present, but how He had planned our lives years before. Our obedience in going to India had allowed Him to fulfill His plan for our lives.

Soon after this, we realized that we had come to a moment of decision. Not only were we down to our last fifty dollars, but the government had now made it clear that, unless we would teach in their schools, cultivate the land, or benefit the country in some tangible way, our visas could not be renewed. It was not at all clear what we should do next, as we had no ticket back to America and no money to buy one.

We did have a ticket back to Karachi, West Pakistan, where our Far Eastern travels had begun. B.G. had prayed before he bought our ticket about how it should be booked and had been led to book us into India and then back to Karachi. "You can always get a refund at the end of the journey," he had assured us, "if you discover that you don't need that extra leg."

We had all but forgotten about that remaining ticket, until it now became necessary to consider all our options. During our short stay in Karachi, we had met many interesting people, including Jerry Longman, a wealthy businessman who had been very keen at the time for us to stay and help the local people build a church. Now, in Madras, as we prayed and pondered about what we should do next, the parting words of this man came back to us. "If God ever calls you to come back, here is my telephone number. Let me know when you are coming, and I will take care of you."

We dug around in our suitcases until we unearthed that business card, and we sent Jerry a telegram. "ARRIVING AT 1 AM NEXT MONDAY MORNING. CAN YOU MEET US?"

CHAPTER NINE

LIFE IN KARACHI

The Karachi Airport was almost deserted and had that bleak, alien atmosphere which seems to brood over many such places in the early hours of the morning. We walked out into the meeting area feeling decidedly jaded after our overnight flight from India. Looking anxiously around we could see no sign of our friend Jerry. We surely would catch the eye of anyone who might have been sent to meet us, but no one seemed to show any interest in us. We expected that any minute someone would come running up to ask our names, but as the minutes turned to hours, we had to face the fact that nobody was coming to meet us. Our plans had somehow gone awry.

A deep sense of desolation overtook us in that moment. Early morning was not the best time to find oneself stranded in a foreign country unable to speak the language and with only fifty dollars left to your name. Even our relatives could not help us. They thought we were still in India.

We have since learned that these are the defining moments of our lives, the true test of our faith. It is so easy to stand up in a church and give a testimony to our total reliance upon God, and it is possible to feel as bold as a lion and to believe that we are almost invincible. However, when all the familiar framework which provides security for our lives is stripped away, and we are left vulnerable in a hostile environment, it is then that our true character is revealed.

That night in Karachi I came face to face with my fears and was challenged as to whether or not I truly believed my life was in God's hands. I wish I could say that I had passed the test with flying colors.

At the moment, there was no alternative but to find a room for what remained of the night. We hailed a taxi and asked the driver to recommend a place for us to stay. Assuming that because we were Americans we must be extremely wealthy, he drove us to an expensive hotel, which we later discovered was frequented by diplomats and the wealthy. Our room was absolutely beautiful, and as we installed ourselves in the plush interior, we realized that we had no idea how much it was going to cost. I found a tariff sheet fixed to the back of the door, and I will never forget the sinking feeling that crept over me as I realized that in the morning we would be penniless. The cost of the room alone was $50, all that we had left.

Part of what happened that night, I am sure, was related to the fact that we were totally exhausted after three months of intensive travelling. We had daily ministered to the needs of the people, continually adjusting to new situations, to the abrupt changes in our diet and to the unhygienic accommodations. Now we were on the verge of destitution in Karachi.

I looked out the window and saw again the many beggars who had made their bed in the streets. Some of them were sheltered in makeshift dwellings made of flimsy cardboard. We had been forced to weave our way

Life In Karachi

through them to gain access to the hotel. Whole families huddled together against the hostility of the night. And suddenly I felt that I just might be joining them soon.

"We're going to die," I cried. "Jerry, we're going to die in this terrible place. And it's so unfair. We've given everything we have, and now we haven't even got the money to telephone home for help. Tomorrow we'll be out there with the beggars. Oh Jerry, I don't want to live with the beggars," I wailed.

My husband looked me directly in the eye and quietly spoke these words: "The Bible says, *'I have been young, and now am old; yet have I not seen the righteous forsaken, nor his seed begging bread.'* "

I can remember thinking somewhat cynically, *Yea, sure.*

"Therefore," Jerry continued, "I believe that God has a way out of this. I don't know exactly what we are going to do, but we are righteous, and we have obeyed God, so He *will* take care of us."

I was grateful for his confidence in God's Word. Our lives now depended on it. Surely God would not leave us homeless on the streets of a Moslem country.

"Come on, let's get some sleep," Jerry suggested.

Still not totally able to take hold of the truth of God's Word, I replied, "Well maybe you can get some sleep, but I don't think I'll be able to. How can we know what will happen tomorrow?"

Eventually, out of sheer exhaustion, we fell asleep.

I awakened, vaguely aware of a very irritating noise which would not stop. It was a ringing sound, and I wished that someone would switch it off so that I could drift back to the bliss of unconsciousness forgetfulness. Finally, we realized that the ringing was right there in our room. We had not heard a telephone for weeks and, as only God knew where we were, we also couldn't imagine who might be calling us. It was Jerry Longman.

As it happened, Jerry's driver had received the telegram, but thinking it to be related to a business deal, he had stuck it in his pocket, meaning to give it to the boss on Monday morning. As intended, that morning he handed Jerry Longman the telegram when he picked him up for work.

Realizing that we must have arrived during the night, Jerry began calling every hotel he could think of in an effort to track us down. What a joy it was to hear his voice!

"You've had a hard night," he said. "Relax and have a nice breakfast, and I will have one of the servants prepare you a room at our place. I will send my driver to pick you up about ten."

Praise God! One moment we had been helpless, scared and on the threshold of penury, and the next we were being told to enjoy breakfast in a grand hotel while servants prepared a room for us and a driver was sent to collect us. God is so gracious, and I felt very humbled that He should be so merciful to me — when I knew I did not deserve it. During the coming days we were treated like royalty, and, although we had no funds of our own, we were living in style in the man's lovely house.

During our time in India, we had been unable to receive mail because we were moving from place to place too often. Our time in Karachi lent us some stability and we were able to reestablish regular contact with home. After a while, our church sent us an offering of $150, and we were able to offer our host something for taking care of us. He was, of course, highly insulted that we would imagine such a thing, but we felt so much better being able to contribute to our keep.

We were quickly able to resume fellowship with two other families we had met on our first visit, the Fredlunds and the Sims, and we began to minister in the area. Our host hired a language teacher so that, ultimately, we would be able to communicate with people directly. And God began to do some wonderful things in that Pakistani community.

Before long, we felt we should have our own place and went looking for something suitable and something we could afford. At one apartment, we had to push hard on the heavy gate in the high security wall to survey the space available. It was extremely small with one bedroom, a lounge and a miniature kitchen which consisted of a sink and a cement slab. There was a little verandah at the front. It wasn't much, but it looked good to us. "We like it," we told the landlord.

"Good. Very good," he said, "I will just need six months' rent in advance."

With that our hopeful spirits plunged. We hadn't realized that advance rent was required. Obviously, it was out of the question.

"Sorry," Jerry told him reluctantly. "We're not able to do that." And we left without wasting more of the man's time.

Walking home, somewhat dejected and disappointed, we, nevertheless, committed everything into God's hands. Money and our lack of it had never been discussed with our host, but he seemed to sense what we were experiencing now and said to us, "I don't know how you are placed for finance, but why don't you let me pay the six months' rent, and then you can pay me back on a monthly basis. How does that sound?"

It sounded good to us. We praised God, moved into our new apartment and set about making it home.

There was no ready-made furniture to be bought in the area, but Jerry Longman insisted on instructing his carpenter to make us a bed and a little cupboard with screens to keep the insects out of our food. We also rented a small refrigerator to keep things cool in the tropical heart. When the refrigerator arrived, I was so anxious to open it and see what it was like. When I enthusiastically pulled open the door, however, I screamed at what I saw. The unit was seething with cockroaches. From that day, one of our major leisurely pursuits was hunting and executing cockroaches.

Chapter Ten

God's Work In Karachi

As the weeks passed, we became more and more absorbed in God's work in Karachi. A church and Sunday school were established in our home, and people were coming to know the Lord. We gradually paid off the six months' advance rent and felt settled in our new home. Everything was looking up.

There were, however, some dangers. We were constantly reminded that we were in a Moslem country and that our home was situated in a predominantly Moslem area of the city. We slowly became aware of undercurrents of hostility around us.

Although we were genuinely grateful for our apartment, there were a few drawbacks. The heat was terribly oppressive. The apartment had a high wall in both front and back and on either side was joined to other buildings, so that there was little room for air to circulate. We needed all the windows and doors open to feel like we could breathe. When we opened them, however, we were invaded by hordes of vicious insects. We decided to enclose our verandah so that we could sit outside sometimes and get some air without being eaten alive.

This simple project proved to be not so simple. First,

it took us several months to save enough to buy the materials. Secondly, it was not easy to buy the wood we needed. We had to make quite a long journey to get it. Next, we had to hire a donkey cart to transport the wood to our place. And finally, Jerry, who had never displayed much of a flair for carpentry, had to figure out how to transform the gnarled and twisted wood into some manageable shape to achieve the desired end.

When the job was completed, however, we were delighted with the results. A professional carpenter might have done it differently, but the construction achieved the purpose for which it had been erected, and that was good enough for us.

About that time, a lovely lady named Phyllis, a tall, dark-haired lady who was full of the love of the Lord, began to attend our church. One day some missionaries we had come to know spoke to us about Phyllis. "We feel that we must warn you about something," they told us. "Phyllis is beginning to trust you and before long she will invite you to her home. You need to prepare yourself for the visit because her husband has leprosy, and he is in a terrible state physically."

Being young and confident of handling anything that came his way, Jerry replied breezily, "We'll be fine. We prayed for lepers many times in India, and we even visited a leper colony. I think we know the kind of thing to expect. We'll cope."

The missionaries eyed each other doubtfully, but went on to explain that Phyllis worked for the government and would lose her job if it was discovered that her husband had leprosy. Therefore, for seventeen years he had been confined to the house. "He is an incredible man though," they went on to say. "In spite of all his sufferings, he has a strong faith and deep devotion to His Lord."

Only a short time elapsed before Phyllis came to visit us one day with a request. "I'd like you to come and meet my husband. He suffers from leprosy. Would that be a problem for you?" she asked anxiously.

We assured her that it was no problem and that we would be delighted to meet him.

She seemed relieved. "That would be wonderful. Maybe we could have a service in our home and pray together. You see, he doesn't get a chance to have any fellowship, and he does love Jesus so much."

"Sure, we would be glad to do that, Phyllis. When would you like us to come?" we asked.

"Well," she paused. "How about now, if you're free." We got ready and left immediately, taking a rickshaw to their house.

It must be said that rickshaw rides in Karachi are not to be undertaken lightly as they can be a terrifying experience. There are several types of rickshaws: rickshaws drawn by people, rickshaws drawn by people on bicycles, and rickshaws pulled by people on motorcycles. There is nothing to differentiate between the three when it comes to evaluating the degree of risk involved in the ride. For me, a rickshaw ride always involved holding my breath and saying a fervent prayer, as entrance into glory always seemed inevitable. I never ceased to be amazed when I found myself alive upon alighting at my destination, although it always took a while for my knees to stop quivering afterward.

We eventually arrived at Phyllis' house, and she led the way inside. My husband walked through the door ahead of me, and I could see his face reflected in a mirror which was hanging on the wall. Total shock and horror registered there, giving me only seconds to prepare for the most terrible sight I had ever seen.

The small room contained twin beds. Phyllis' husband, dressed in an open-necked shirt and dark trousers, sat on one of the beds. His skin was bleached a strange, almost ethereal white, and a dark crater existed in the center of his face where once his nose had been. All that remained of his ears were grotesque lumps, and there were just gnarled stumps where his fingers had been eaten away. I am ashamed to say that a wave of nausea swept over me as I looked at this poor man whose body was being slowly devastated by this hideous disease.

It was with some relief that I realized that the man was blind, and therefore unable to see our reactions or appreciate the extent of his own deformity. We swiftly regained our composure and, as we began to see beyond external appearances, we realized that here was an intelligent man with a heart bursting with love for God.

After this initial visit, we returned each week to have dinner with Phyllis and her husband, to pray with them and to share the Word of God. On each visit, we would talk about what God was doing in the church and about other matters, as well. As we met thus, week after week, a deep love and respect developed between us. I must admit that I wondered if we might catch the leprosy but, praise God, we never did. We grew to admire the grace and courage of this man which enabled him to triumph over the most unimaginable agony and suffering. It was a privilege to know him.

Returning home the night of our first visit, still shaken by our first sight of this man, we understood why the other missionaries had taken such trouble to warn us about what we would encounter in Phyllis' home. However, there were more shocks in store for us that day.

As we arrived home, we were met with a scene of chaos. Our front gate was open and huge stones were strewn everywhere. All the screening we had so painstakingly erected on the veranda had been torn down and lay in a twisted, useless heap. Worse yet, a chilling message was scrawled on our doorstep: FORBIDDEN TO ENTER THIS HOUSE.

Numbed and exhausted by the day's events, we went inside realizing that, had we been at home, we could easily have been killed. God had protected us that night, and we were grateful.

In the days ahead, we had many decisions to make. It was obvious that the working of God in our midst would produce further opposition, but we decided to go ahead with the church and Sunday school, relying on God's help and protection.

Difficulties would soon come from another quarter. Without warning, we received a letter one morning from our home church saying that they had taken a decision to cut our monthly support from $150 to $100s. We were shocked and, together, we sat down and wept.

Someone had advised our pastor that we didn't need more than $100 a month, that we could live well in Karachi on that amount. Somehow the impression had been given that while the church made sacrifices to support us, we were living in the lap of luxury.

The person who took it upon himself to do us this great favor didn't even know us and had no idea what we were really doing in Karachi.

The truth was that we were barely making ends meet

with the offering we were getting. We had rent to pay, food bills, transportation costs to remote areas, and we were buying materials for teaching the children in our Sunday school, just for starters. We didn't know anyone back home who was living on a level lower than us. How could anyone begrudge us $150 a month? We felt wounded and betrayed.

Our heartbreak lasted only a little while, and when we determined to go forward — whatever happened — God turned the situation around, and eventually that $50 per month was restored. Although the criticism of our expenditures seemed very personal at the time, we should never have worried, for God provided our needs in many wonderful ways day-by-day.

I remember one particularly difficult moment when our money had run out, and we had nothing to eat. Right then, the future looked rather bleak. Soon, however, a large envelope arrived in the mail. It had originally been sent to India and had chased us across the subcontinent.

The envelope was from a classmate at Zion and contained, among other things, a batch of interesting newspaper clippings. Buried in the middle of all those clippings was $150 in cash. It was a miracle that the package ever reached us in the first place, but the fact that the cash was still there, intact, was altogether amazing. And it couldn't have arrived at a better moment. Over and over again God made a way for us where there seemed to be no way.

Chapter Eleven

Our Love For Children

One day a friend asked me if I would like to accompany her to a village where she was going to speak in a ladies' meeting. I was enthusiastic about this opportunity and together we braved the hazardous rickshaw ride.

We made our way along a narrow dirt road toward the mud huts of the village, flicking away the persistent flies that buzzed around our heads. The stench from the open sewers was nauseating and the heat almost unbearable.

Each hut in the village was surrounded by a small mud wall, and sewage flowed down an open ditch outside. We picked our way carefully on foot to avoid falling into one of those ditches.

In the first house we entered we found a tiny skeleton of a child lying listlessly on a simple cot. Several other local ladies were there. As I looked at that sick child, a sudden recognition of the agony, hunger, distress and desperate struggle for survival these simple village people faced every day, swept over me.

No one in the village spoke English, so my friend had to tell me what was being said. "Gail, she wants you to pray for her child," she said. "She has been sick for some weeks now and is getting weaker every day. I don't pray for the sick myself, but I know that you do, so please go ahead if you would like to."

We later discovered that the child was a measles victim and had developed pneumonia. Poor diet and lack of medical care and attention had robbed her body of the ability to resist.

I went near to the cot and took the child in my arms. As I did this, she drew in a gulp of air and suddenly died in my arms. My friend saw what happened and spoke to me quickly and quietly: "Gail, you must not show any emotion. If you do, they will think you have killed the child. Lay her carefully back on the bed. Then, I'll tell the lady that her baby has died, nothing more. Then we must get out of here as fast as we can, or we may lose our lives."

I felt totally bewildered, shocked and frightened. I had never seen anyone die before, and to have a child die in my arms was more than I could quickly comprehend. If our lives were in danger on top of that, I wasn't sure what we should do. As my friend was a more experienced missionary, I mechanically obeyed her instructions. I carefully laid the child back on the cot, then listened as the other missionary spoke to the mother of the child. I was prepared to beat a hasty retreat.

I was caught off guard, however, by what happened next. The mother let out an ear-splitting scream, and then the other Pakistani women in the house began to wail and scream in a terrifying cacophony of grief. It was all extremely unnerving, so we quickly took our leave.

As we left the hut, we had to pass by a line of men sitting silently outside smoking their pipes. Their presence suddenly seemed very threatening and, as we zigzagged through the village and back to the rickshaw, I half expected to see those men pursuing us brandishing knives or other weapons. Our plan to attend the ladies' meeting was abandoned as we made our quick escape.

On the way back home, my friend tried to explain to me why she had reacted as she did. The village people were, she said, extremely superstitious. The fact that I had touched the child might lead them to believe that I had put a curse on her and caused her to die.

It was the custom of the women to mourn a death in the village, and it was the custom of the men to wait silently outside until it was time for the burial. Clad in a simple white garment, the body would be carried to the local burial ground and laid to rest.

As for me, I cried all the way home, suddenly overwhelmed by all the poverty, grief and danger of this country in which we were living.

When I got back, Jerry greeted me cheerily. "How did it go?"

With this, I burst into tears again and, between sobs I tried to tell him how the little child had died in my arms. I would never forget that face, and it changed my life forever.

There have been many high spots in our missionary experience, great miracles of healing, deliverance and the provision of God, but that day began in me a process of identifying with the terrible anguish and heartache of the people. I began to feel the pain, the loss and the hunger in the people I met, and my priorities began to change.

In the Western world we all seem to be totally dominated by the pursuit of things: a beautiful home, an expensive car. As I began to feel people's pain, these things sank very low on my list of priorities.

The eighteen months we spent in India and Pakistan brought a new maturity to my life, and I learned so many things. I left America as a mere child, but I returned as a woman.

During our time in Karachi, I suffered another miscarriage. Although we loved children so much, it looked increasingly as if we might not have any of our own. Looking back, I can see the hand of God in all this, but at the moment I was living it, it was a devastating experience.

Children were also very important to the Pakistanis and Indians. If a wife could not give her husband a child, he had every right to divorce her and marry another who could. All he had to do was say the words, "I divorce you," then turn in a circle, and the deed was legally accomplished. Many Indian and Pakistani women, desperate not to lose their husbands, pleaded with me to pray for them so that they could bear a child. Later many returned to tell me they were indeed pregnant and, when eight or nine months had passed, they would arrive, with great pride, to show me their offspring.

I found it very difficult to understand why God was honoring my prayers for other women, while I remained childless, and sometimes I even felt angry with Him about the whole affair. Deep inside I would cry out in anguish: "Why God? Why can't You give me a child too?"

During one of those particularly hard times, we met some Swedish missionaries who ran a children's home. They had several small babies to care for, and it proved to be more than they could handle. There were always piles of diapers and other clothes to be washed and formula to be prepared from canned milk and crushed biscuits. Jerry and I decided to lend them a hand. Our work with those orphaned babies proved to be very therapeutic for both of us.

Our Love For Children

One day we arrived at the home to find that the lady in charge had suffered a serious heart attack. She was so important to the operation that this left the home seriously understaffed. Jerry and I agreed to try to take up some of the slack. We now began to go in every day and, for several weeks, actually stayed right there.

Eventually, however, this added burden began to have an adverse effect on our own ministry, and we decided that we had to cut back. If it would help, we told our friends, we would be glad to take one of the babies home with us. They were delighted.

It was difficult to decide which child to take. I wanted to take a gorgeous little girl named Elizabeth, but Jerry had become attached to a baby boy named Salamat. As a compromise, we ended up taking two babies back with us to our tiny apartment.

The wonderful baby equipment that is common now in our Western world, was unknown in Pakistan. We made beds for the babies from dresser drawers and improvised in other ways so that we could properly care for them. Many very funny moments occurred in our new role as foster parents.

For instance, Jerry and I had an agreement: if Elizabeth woke up during the night, I would feed her, change her and put her back to bed. Jerry would do the same for Salamat. I had grown up with plenty of babies around, but Jerry, as an only child, hadn't had those experiences. Boy did he get his eyes open fast! Changing diapers turned out to be a far more complicated process than he had imagined!

The children stayed with us just one week, but it was a very interesting and enlightening week.

CHAPTER TWELVE

PEOPLE OF "ONE HEART"

The relationship we had forged with the missionary families in Karachi brought us great joy. As the Scriptures declare:

And the multitude of them that believed were of one heart and of one soul: Acts 4:32

The Sims had two boys, David and Jonathan, and the Fredlunds a boy, also called David, and a girl, Anita. These children became very important to us, and we had wonderful times together. We were young and foolish, and they genuinely seemed to enjoy our company. When the Sims family invited us to join them and their dog Trixie for a holiday on the Indian Ocean, we didn't need much persuasion. We had been working very hard, and some rest and relaxation was badly needed.

They had arranged to use a cottage on the beach owned by the Baptist missionaries, and the description of it sounded idyllic. Thoughts of gentle sea breezes, seaside scenes and of being able to collapse with nothing to do except enjoy ourselves were very intoxicating. The reality, however, was a little different.

The first morning in the beachfront cabin, I awoke

early to the gentle, soothing sound of lapping water. Looking out the window, I suddenly realized that we were totally surrounded by water. "Jerry! Jerry! Wake up!" I screamed. "We've floated out to sea."

Actually, we had been caught by high tide, and when the tide went out, we would be back to normal. "Normal," however, was not what I imagined. Staying in a crude hut with no running water and no electricity was not my idea of the perfect vacation.

Another morning I awoke to find a rat standing on the sacred territory of Jerry's pillow, twitching its whiskers inches from his face. I let out a bloodcurdling scream which sent the offending animal running for cover and brought Jerry to an instant sitting position. "What is it?" he asked, startled.

"A rat, Jerry. An enormous rat," I answered. "It had the audacity to run across your pillow. That's it! I've had enough of this place. It's time to go home."

The boys pleaded with us to stay and tried to divert my thoughts from the brazen rat by getting us a camel ride on the beach. This experience turned out to be nearly as alarming as the rat episode, but we ended up finishing out the holiday.

The Sims and Fredlunds have since retired after many fruitful years of missionary service, but we still keep in touch with them. Sometimes these "on-the-job" relationships are deeper than those shared with members of one's own family. We shared the same heartbeat and vision and knew the same hurts, pain and frustrations of preaching the Gospel in a foreign land. Bonds forged like this are not easily broken, and we praise God for these relationships which were so important to us.

After eighteen months away from home, Jerry and I

both had a strong sense that God was showing us to return to America. This was, for us, a most unexpected turn of events. We had always believed that when anyone went abroad for missionary work, it was forever. Most missionaries we had known served for four or five years, took a short break at home and then went right back to the field. We were learning not to make commitments beyond the present vision God had given us.

It was difficult to answer those who demanded a more concrete reason for our departure. We were not sure exactly what God had in mind. Just a few days after our return to America, however, we heard the news that the Karachi suburb where we lived had been bombed, and that India and Pakistan were now at war. We were never able to determine if the actual building we were living in was bombed, or if we might have lost our lives if we had stayed on. We could only conclude that God had spared us by getting us out of the city just in time.

This left us with another question: *What now?* Surely God must have some other purpose for us to fulfil.

CHAPTER THIRTEEN

FILLING EMPTY ARMS

A fter we returned home, we got busy minis-
tering wherever doors opened to us. Eventually we pastored in several areas and also
taught in Bible schools. All during this time, it continued to bother me that we hadn't yet been able to have
children of our own. It just didn't seem fair to me.
Women are made to have children, so why couldn't I
have one? I asked God the question many times, but still
couldn't seem to receive an answer that satisfied me. I
believed in the scriptural promise:

> *Lo, children are an heritage of the LORD: and the fruit
> of the womb is his reward. As arrows are in the hand
> of a mighty man; so are children of the youth. Happy
> is the man that hath his quiver full of them: they shall
> not be ashamed, but they shall speak with the enemies
> in the gate.*   Psalms 127:3-5

I felt like I was trusting God for a child and couldn't
understand why He didn't give me *"the desires of [my]
heart":*

> *Trust (lean on, rely on, and be confident) in the Lord,*

*and do good; so shall you dwell in the land and feed
surely on His faithfulness, and truly you shall be fed.
Delight yourselves also in the Lord, and He will give
you the desires of your heart. Commit your way to
the Lord, roll and repose each care of your load on
Him; trust (lean on, rely on and be confident) also in
Him, and He will bring it to pass.*

Psalm 37:3-5, Amplified

What was I doing wrong? God had even promised
that I would be the mother of many nations. What did
that mean? I couldn't even be the mother of one child,
let alone a nation or nations. Was there something wrong
with me? One day, when this raw wound inside had
opened up once again and I was sobbing my heart out
in Jerry's arms, he said to me, "Gail, why don't we adopt
a baby?"

I recoiled like a released metal spring and, consumed
by a sudden surge of anger, replied emphatically, "No! I
won't adopt a baby."

"But Gail, we both love children, and if we can't have
our own baby, surely adoption would be the next best
thing."

"No!" I insisted. "If God doesn't want to give me a
child then I will just do without. If I can't have it my
way, then I don't want it any way." And with that I
stalked out of the room, bristling with rage because I
believed God had failed me.

Over the years, Jerry tried to talk to me about adoption many times, but my response was always negative.
Then, one day, God began to change my heart. A distraught mother approached us while we were pastoring
in New York. "Please, will you try to help our daugh-

ter," she pleaded. She had often requested prayer for her daughter during our services, but this plea seemed to be different. "She once knew the Lord, but she is now far from God, pregnant, and about to become an unmarried mother. We're at the end of our tether," the woman said. "She won't listen to us, but maybe she would take notice if you talked to her. We don't know what to do."

My heart went out to this woman. It was clear that she was very distressed about the whole situation, but as I thought about this girl, all my old feelings of injustice came to the surface yet again. Why should I, of all people, have to pray for an unmarried mother? Why should I have to care for a girl who had brought this situation on herself by her willful sin? I considered myself worthy of having a child, yet I was unable to give birth, while this unmarried woman, who was in totally inappropriate circumstances for bringing up children, was about to bring another human being into the world. I was very reluctant to get involved. We were the pastors of the church, however, so we agreed to visit the daughter, to pray with her and to counsel her.

The girl was adamant that she wanted to keep the baby despite the sustained efforts of social workers to persuade her to give the child up for adoption. Her time came and the baby was born.

We went to the hospital to visit mother and child (a son, Matthew) and took with us a gift, a little yellow jumpsuit. We had no way of knowing that this was his first outfit.

We continued to take an interest in Matthew and his mother after they left the hospital and prayed for them regularly. And they needed prayer. The mother saw nothing wrong with carting her young son from barroom to barroom, as she settled back into a totally godless lifestyle. When she asked me one day if I could look after him while she looked for a job, I agreed out of pity for the child, and when the job hunting became prolonged, I didn't mind. I had grown to love Matthew. He had become firmly entwined in our lives and to lose him would devastate me.

My father-in-law who had strongly advised us against adoption, fell in love with Matthew and urged us to make our relationship with him permanent. We agreed and prayed that we could somehow make that desire a reality.

One day I heard Jerry's car turn into the drive. Matthew didn't stir from his nap. I felt a surge of love for him as I looked at his peaceful face. What a blessing he was!

The key turned in the lock and Jerry called out, "Gail, we've got a visitor."

When I went into the other room to see who had come, a twinge of anxiety jerked at my heart. It was Matthew's mother and I had been fearing that she might return to say that she was taking him away forever. But my fears turned to joy.

After we had chatted for a while, the woman suddenly looked me straight in the eye and asked, "How would you like to adopt Matthew?"

I was so thrilled that I found myself tongue-tied and unable to respond properly. Without waiting for my answer, she continued, "I love him, but I recognize that I can't care for him properly. I can't give him what he needs. I see that you love him too, and I know that you can bring him up in a much better environment."

She continued to speak, this time with a slightly distant look in her dark eyes. "You know, when I was carrying him, I had a dream. In my dream I had given birth to a little boy, and I felt that God told me to call him Matthew. When he was actually born I called him Matthew because I knew that was the name chosen for him by God." That day we made arrangements to legally adopt Matthew and raise him up as our own son.

The name Matthew means "gift of God." It didn't seem to be a very appropriate name for the son of an unwed mother, but Matthew proved to be an incredibly precious gift to us. He brought such joy into our lives and helped to ease the pain of our childless years. He grew to be a loving son and, even now that he is a man, we have a bond of love and respect more precious than gold.

With Matthew's adoption, my resistance to the process was broken and we now decided to become foster parents, as well. Over the coming years, many children, usually with deep emotional needs, were sent to join our family. When one little six-year-old came to live with us, I remember reaching out to hug him and saying, "How about giving me a kiss?"

He looked up at me quizzically and replied, "What's a kiss?"

I was so shocked that a child born into enlightened America could have no experience of a mother's kiss of love and acceptance. We shared the Gospel with all the children who stayed with us, and some of them came to know God for themselves.

Kenny was ten when he came to us. He was filled with anger, bitterness and hatred, and it all overflowed violently into his behavior. But God touched his life, and he is now married with three lovely daughters of his own and is serving God as an elder in his local church. Although Kenny is not a Rozell by name, I still count him as one of my sons.

Since I had a deep desire to have twin daughters, we decided to try and adopt them. When we asked a social worker how we would go about that, she rolled her red pencil between her fingers and looked very dubious. "I'm afraid it is very difficult to adopt twins, Mrs. Rozell," she answered.

"How difficult?" I inquired.

"Well, if I tell you that I have been in this job for seventeen years and in that time I have seen only one set of twins adopted, then you'll have some idea of the problem. I am sorry to discourage you, but there is a long waiting list of couples anxious to adopt twins, so, even if they are available for adoption, you would not be eligible for a very long time."

We continued to pray that if God wanted us to have twins He would work it out. If not, we would be grateful for whoever He sent to us.

About a year later the telephone rang. Matthew was by this time four years old. My heart quickened its pace when I realized it was the social welfare department. "Mrs. Rozell, do you still want twins?" the lady on the other end of the line asked.

"Yes we do," I replied immediately.

"Well, we have a set of girls, and we believe they would be ideal for you."

"What about the other people on the list you told us about?"

"Well yes," she answered, "there are other people ahead of you on the list, but we still feel that the twins should come to you. We are allowed some discretionary placements."

This was God's way of answering our prayer. I have often wondered if the twins, Gerrilynn and Cheryl, might have had a godly grandmother who prayed that they would be placed in a Christian home. I will probably never know if this was the case, but I do know that right from the start the hand of God was on their lives.

Now we had a son and two daughters, and I cannot imagine a family anywhere on earth loving each other as much as we did and still do. I believe God handpicked these children and brought them to our home. It has been so thrilling to watch them grow up wanting to serve God. We have all been involved together on many occasions in making Jesus Christ known to people and there is no joy quite like that.

Just because we now had three adopted children didn't mean that we had given up having some of our own. That desire was still strong within me. It came as a shock, therefore, when I started hemorrhaging one night in church. Someone helped me to get home, and eventually I was taken to hospital, where I discovered that I had had my third miscarriage.

Once again I was plunged back into a dark pit of depression and despair. I had not even known that I was pregnant, but I was soon aware that I had still not resolved this problem of my childlessness — spiritually or emotionally. My three adopted children had brought enormous joy to my life, and some of the pain of the past was soothed but, after this third failure to carry a child, I knew that many things had been pushed down into a cellar area of my life. Now the struggle had burst up to the surface once more and could not be ignored.

All the turmoil, agony, angry questions and confusion started again.

Basically, I was still unable to understand and accept that God was saying "No" to my prayer for a child. Why had He allowed me to become pregnant again when He knew the baby would be lost? Was God playing cruel games with me?

I was so upset with this turn of events that as soon as I felt a little better, I decided to go away for a few days and try to sort out my thoughts and to come to terms with my loss. The more I thought about what had happened, the less I understood what God was doing. I thought it was part of the "deal" that if I obeyed God things would go my way. I had no understanding of the role suffering would play in my life or what it truly meant to receive *the desires of [my] heart.* I felt let down by God because He didn't seem to be considering my feelings.

I had a lot to learn about "my rights." Was God some sort of slot machine, placed in our lives for our convenience? Did I just have to insert a prayer and press the right button to get what I wanted from Him?

After a few days of pondering these kinds of thoughts, one night, about 2:00 a.m., I came to the end of myself and surrendered my will fully to God. "Father, forgive me," I prayed. "Forgive me for wanting my own way. Maybe I will never understand what You are trying to accomplish in me, but I do trust You. I trust that You know what You are doing. I give up the fight, and I hand it all over to You." Something lifted from my shoulders in that moment and, although I was drained and exhausted, I knew that I had entered into a new phase of liberation regarding this sensitive area of my life.

Filling Empty Arms

Today I can honestly say that I do have peace, joy and no regrets when I consider this issue which has been the source of so much inner grief for me through the years. From that moment on I was able to move forward into the life that God had for me. God has filled my empty arms in the way that He saw best, and I am grateful.

I would like to challenge others who have struggled and rebelled against God, as I did when He denied my request for children of my own. You may not understand God's ways, but take a chance on trusting Him. Obey Him, and He will certainly give you the desires of your heart. Be prepared, however, for some shocks concerning the way He chooses to do this. In our pain and distress there often seem to be no alternatives, no viable options, but God always thinks of ways to do things we would never consider ourselves. The result is the best for us, a life of fulfillment in Him. In the end, I knew that His promise was true:

They that sow in tears shall reap in joy. He that goeth forth and weepeth, bearing precious seed, shall doubtless come again with rejoicing, bringing his sheaves with him. **Psalms 126:5-6**

CHAPTER FOURTEEN

SAVING THE WORLD, AND LOSING YOUR FAMILY

As our children developed, one of my greatest concerns was that I would not become so absorbed in the ministry that I could not notice if my own children began slipping away from their spiritual life. I had seen too many children with parents in the ministry who eventually rejected the faith their parents taught. Some of them concluded that they were unwanted and of little value to their parents because those parents were always too busy to listen to them. Many of them became bitter because they believed the church or ministry had stolen their parents, leaving them virtual orphans, denied the rights of a child to be loved, nurtured and supported. I was determined not to let that happen.

I have always loved the description in Proverbs 31 of a godly wife and mother. Conscious that I did not possess many of the attributes shown there, I cried out to God to teach me how to be righteous and loving. Although I made many mistakes and now wish that I had approached some things differently, I constantly found myself reaching out to God for help and He was always there. "Lord," I prayed, "please don't let me save the world and lose my own children." I wanted my children to *rise and call me blessed,* not because I was on some ego trip, but because I wanted to know that with God's help, I had not failed as a mother.

My children were just like other children and were sometimes fractious from the moment they opened their eyes.

"He's got my doll."

"Give it back, Matthew."

"Come and get it."

"Give it to me."

"Give it to me."

Then came loud screams and the sound of running feet.

"Mom, he's got my doll and he won't give it back."

"Matthew, for goodness sake give her back her doll. Now! This minute!"

"Why should I?"

"Because I'm telling you to. And don't you dare use that tone of voice with me again."

They sometimes seemed to be totally impossible, and I was exasperated with them for behaving like spoiled brats and exasperated with myself for being the "failed mother of the year." But in the midst of my anger and frustration, I would hear the Holy Spirit whisper in my ear: "It's you. Your attitude is wrong. If you get your attitude sorted out, then the children will be fine."

I had to repent and ask God to change my attitude, and gradually the situation would improve and harmony would reign once more in our home — until next time.

Sometimes I was too hard on them, and sometimes I was too soft on them. Often I sinned in the way I handled them, and I had to come to God in repentance and ask for His forgiveness. At those times I also had to ask *their* forgiveness. If I shed many tears during the years I had no children, I shed even more tears as I struggled to learn to be something approaching a godly mother.

I have never felt the need to try to pretend that we were somehow perfect, as some Christian leaders do. We are all flesh and blood, and all parents make many mistakes. To see an occasional problem might actually be an encouragement to those around us. Then they would know there is hope for them too.

Every parent struggles with toddler tantrums in the supermarket and moody teenagers who find everything boring. Those continually faced with the ideal Christian family smiling down smugly from the dizzy heights of their pedestal of perfection might actually be blessed by observing an occasional harsh word or a full-blown argument. If they are constantly confronted by perfection, they may sink further into condemnation because they seem incapable of matching the standards of their leaders.

As Matthew moved into his teenage years, Jerry and I often discussed what we could do to keep our children close to God. On one occasion, when this topic was under consideration, we were on our way to a church service. In the course of that service, a man who knew nothing of our conversation about our family, brought us a word from God. He said: "The heritage of a righteous man is righteous children. If you will be righteous, then God is going to give you righteous children."

We had tried to always live what we preached to the children. We had seen too many promote one set of values from the pulpit and operate according to a completely different code of conduct at home. Those double standards often caused children to turn their backs on God's Kingdom. Our children made us proud, and we could identify with the words of the Apostle John to Gaius:

> *I have no greater joy than to hear that my children*
> *walk in truth.*   3 John 1:4

My handpicked children are all adults now, and how I praise God that they all love Him. Although they may not always have understood or agreed with our decisions as parents, they were not deterred from developing their own relationship with God. I know that this is the result of God's grace and intervention after much anguished intercession and not the product of any natural talent for parenting.

As my own life had been shaped by the spiritual inheritance which was passed from my grandmother to her son and then to me, Jerry and I, in turn, have had the immense joy of positively affecting the spiritual development of our children. I hope that we, too, will be able to have input into the lives of any grandchildren we may have in the future.

The psalmist has written:

> *But the steadfast love of the Lord is from everlasting*
> *to everlasting upon those who fear him, and his right-*
> *eousness to children's children, to those who keep his*
> *covenant and remember to do his commandments.*
>   Psalm 103:17-18, NRSV

How exciting it is that every ordinary person committed to living in single-minded devotion to God's laws has spiritual treasures to pass on to the next generation. Each individual man or woman who is prepared to put God first can make a significant contribution to the growth of the Kingdom of Heaven, not only in their own time, but also in succeeding generations, if they teach their children God's ways.

If compromise and neglect tend to become hallmarks of our behavior, therefore, we must consider the implications, not only for our own walk with God, but also for our diminished ability to pass on an heritage of life to the next generation. Our responsibility to our children should always be a high priority in our lives as Christians.

CHAPTER FIFTEEN

GOD'S DAILY PROVISION FOR US

Things did not always go well financially for us, even when we were serving God in America. Once, when Jerry was pastoring a small church, we seemed to come to the end of our resources.

"I'm going out tomorrow to look for a job," Jerry announced. "I can't sit here any longer and watch my family suffer."

I felt like saying, "Amen, do it." Instead I replied, "Is that what God has told you to do?"

"No, I can't say it's what God has told me to do, but I have no choice. We have to provide for our children."

There was more to the story. The Holy Spirit had shown Jerry that some of the men in leadership in the church needed to clean up their lives and be better examples for others to follow. He had suspended them from their leadership positions until they could get things sorted out. This inevitably caused tension, and we became the scapegoats for people's anger.

It had been very painful for Jerry to discipline these people. He would rather not have done it, but he knew he would be disobedient to the teaching of Scripture if he just tried to ignore the situation. On top of the pain of taking the required action, now we were faced with a new situation. Some of the best tithe-paying members had stopped giving in the offerings, and that can be very serious for a small congregation.

We had been living in a lovely home and driving a fine automobile, but now we found ourselves unable to pay our basic bills. I had always believed that Christians who live by faith should pay their bills on time and thus live beyond reproach, yet our mortgage was three months in arrears; we were being threatened with the disconnection of the utilities, and we had been unable to pay the latest telephone bill. We had reached the stage where we didn't even have a loaf of bread or a box of salt in the house.

We cried out to God in great distress: "God, we stood up for righteousness. We stood up for the principles in Your Word, and the people have stopped supporting us. Please help us. We don't know what to do."

When we went to church on Sunday, the attendance seemed quite good, and we were hopeful that there would be a decent offering from which our salary could be paid, but we were disappointed. It was the smallest offering the church had ever received since we had been there. That day we returned home with sinking hearts. If things did not improve soon, we would be unable to feed our children, and the house would be repossessed. We had never been in such a serious situation before — at least in this land of plenty.

We prayed earnestly to God that evening: "God, please hear us. Our testimony in the community will be ruined. You know this whole situation has only arisen because we have tried to be faithful to Your Word. Lord, provide for our children. Please help us."

The next day I backed the car out of the garage and drove down the road to the supermarket to spend the last twenty dollar bill we had left. As I reached a certain stop sign I felt as if God was saying to me, "Gail, I want you to praise Me."

I would like to be able to say that I immediately responded and began to worship, secure in the knowledge that God would not let us down. Instead I was cross. "Lord, this is not fair. Every time we stand up for what is right we have to go through all this painful persecution. I can't praise You right now."

I continued to moan and complain like the children of Israel in the wilderness, but God said to me once again, "Gail, praise Me." I pretended that I had not heard and kept going.

When God spoke to me for the third time, I did begrudgingly begin to praise Him, although it was only lip service and not from my heart. Slowly, however, something began to stir within me, and faith in God's power to provide increased.

I was able to pray, "Lord, if we do what is right, I know that You will make a way where there seems to be no way. I'm sorry for moaning. Thank You. I know that You are my Provider."

I became so engrossed in praising God that I overshot the turn for the bargain supermarket where I usually purchased my groceries. I stopped in front of another store which was more expensive, but I concluded that since I could only afford a few items, it would not make a significant difference to the bill if I shopped there. Still praising God, I seized my basket and entered the supermarket — totally unaware of the surprises God had prepared for me.

Supermarkets are not generally renowned as locations for the spectacular display of God's power, but that is what took place in that particular store on that particular day. A man in a white meat-cutter's jacket stood inside the door. I noticed that he was picking up one or two items from the shelf and repricing them. I was surprised to discover that a box of salt had been marked down to a penny. Canned hams now only cost a few cents each.

This seemed crazy. The prices I was seeing were ridiculously low. To my amazement I noticed that the man seemed to be repricing all the items I needed most. Drawn as if by a magnet, I followed him up and down the aisles filling my basket with unbelievably low-priced goods.

"All bread and pastry in this store will be reduced to ten cents for the next five minutes," came an announcement over the loudspeaker. Hardly daring to believe what was happening, I ran over to the shelves and began filling my cart with jelly donuts, cream puffs, large loaves of bread and crusty rolls. This was wonderful!

I managed to find a half gallon of ice-cream marked down to fifty cents and, having a great weakness for coffee, I went to investigate the situation in that department. Sure enough, Mr. White-coat had passed that way with his price-slashing pen while I had been stocking up on bread and pastries and I got an unbelievable deal on some coffee.

While I was picking out the coffee, I noticed a small interesting-looking piece of paper lying on the shelf. I picked it up and discovered that it was a coupon which further reduced the price of the coffee, making it virtually free. There were no other coupons in sight, so I concluded that it was probably out of date. Nevertheless, I took it with me to the checkout counter along with my overflowing cart.

As I waited in the line at the checkout counter, I began to panic, fearful that it was somehow a mistake. Some of the items I had taken from the shelves were things I would not normally buy because they were too expensive. Would I now be presented with a bill I couldn't pay?

When it came my turn, the girl looked at the coffee coupon and asked, "Where did you get this?"

"It was on the shelf with the coffee," I said. "Is it valid?"

"Oh yes, it's valid, but I have never seen one like this before, although I've worked here for years. Were there any more like this?"

"No," I responded, "that seemed to be the only one."

When I pulled out into traffic that day, I had change from my twenty dollars and a back seat loaded with groceries. Needing no prompting now to praise God, I rejoiced at full volume all the way home. "Jerry, come and give me a hand," I called as I started to unload my purchases.

He appeared and gasped as he saw all the bags of provisions I had brought. "Gail, where on earth did you get all this food?" he asked. "You didn't have enough money for a fraction of this." Maybe, fleetingly, he wondered if his wife had done the unthinkable and resorted to shoplifting.

I began to tell him the remarkable story of what had transpired at the supermarket and when I had finished

I saw that his eyes were full of tears. "Gail, God sent an angel today to provide for us."

Angels had not featured in my experience or my thinking until that day, and I wasn't quite sure what had happened. All I know is that, just as God sent a raven to feed Elijah, He had sent a man in a white coat to a local supermarket so that our children could have food to eat.

Later that same morning a lady from our church came to visit us. Handing us a large check, she explained that it was the tithe of an inheritance she had recently received. "God told me to give this to you. I was going to wait until Sunday, but He woke me up this morning and told me that you needed it immediately and that I should give it to you today." That check covered our outstanding mortgage payments and all our other unpaid bills. In the space of a few hours all our debts had been cleared and our cupboards were stocked with food.

I was so glad that the Holy Spirit enabled me to praise God even when it was the last thing I wanted to do at the moment. If I had continued to refuse the Spirit's prompting, surely that day might well have turned out very differently.

Our God is able. He can be trusted one hundred percent to keep His Word. Just as a little child does not question the things his parents tell him, so we must not question the words of God.

On another occasion, God's care for us was demonstrated in yet another unusual way. We had decided to build a new home. The bank had approved the loan, we had sought the services of a local builder and settled on a design, and the project was ready to go forward. All that remained to be done was sign the contract. But suddenly, for no apparent reason, we began to have second thoughts.

What was wrong we were not sure. We just felt uncomfortable with the situation. Could we be moving outside the will of God by building in this location? We didn't know. When we discussed our feelings with the builder, he was very disgusted with us.

"But I don't understand," he protested. "Why can't you go ahead with the house?"

Since we were not sure ourselves what we were feeling, it wasn't easy to answer that question. In the end, we told him, "We just don't feel that it's the right thing for us to do now."

"Oh, come on, there must be some logical reason," he insisted. "You were so enthusiastic a week or so ago." He could barely conceal his anger, and who could blame him? I was disappointed too. What was God doing in our lives?

A year later we were moving into a new home built for us by a different builder in an entirely different location. Later we discovered that the builder involved in the first plan had been found to be a crook, a liar and a shoddy workman. The houses he had built were already deteriorating, had faulty sewers and many other structural problems. How grateful we were to God that He had saved us from the financial disaster of owning such a home.

The prophet Isaiah promised:

If ye be willing and obedient, ye shall eat the good of the land: but if ye refuse and rebel, ye shall be devoured with the sword. Isaiah 1:19-20

Thank God we had taken the right approach to our new home, and thank God for His faithfulness.

Many years ago I heard the following declaration of intent and it so struck a chord in my heart that I made it my own:

> *"When I face a mountain I will not quit.*
> *I will climb over it.*
> *I will go around it.*
> *I will tunnel under it, or*
> *With the help of God,*
> *I will stand and turn it into a gold mine."*

CHAPTER SIXTEEN

INDIA REVISITED

One day God spoke to Jerry about going back to India. "God is going to take us back to India," he announced. "I don't know yet if we will be just visiting there to preach, or if we are to return there on a long-term basis to work as missionaries again, but we will definitely be going back."

It was now 1975 and more than ten years had passed since we left America as vulnerable young people to begin our first missionary enterprise. The thought of a permanent return to India with three young children was, to say the least, daunting, but we had renewed our vow to God to go wherever He wanted to send us, and now we set ourselves to pray for His direction.

Late one night the telephone rang. I heard Jerry say the name Ernest, and it registered that he seemed surprised to hear from the man. I was trying to think who he might be talking to. "I don't need to pray about it," I heard him say. "God has already told me that I will be coming, so just send the details."

When he had put down the receiver, he filled me in on all the missing details. The Ernest in question was originally from India but had studied with us at Zion. God had then used this man in a powerful way in his home country, and he had built a large number of churches and started many orphanages there. He was now a nationally known Christian leader and had called from India to invite Jerry to speak at a convention he was holding in February. We would soon be on our way for a six-week preaching stint in India, during which we would minister to some twenty thousand people. Matthew, who was ten at the time, accompanied us on this trip, and God used the experience to plant many good seeds in his life.

At first, I had been opposed to his going. I was well acquainted with the hazards of India, and I feared that Matthew would become seriously ill or even die if we exposed him to the tropical diseases and generally unhealthy conditions that existed there. Losing him, after waiting so long for a child, would be more than I could bear. But as it became clear to me that God wanted us to take him, I had to put his life in God's hands and trust God that all would be well.

While we were in India, Matthew's faith was stirred. One day he said to me, "Mom, I know that God wants me to be baptized." He had been reading the Bible and discovered the passage which speaks of the three witnesses: the Spirit, the water and the blood. Knowing that he had been washed in the blood of Jesus and filled with His Spirit, he now wanted to be baptized in water. And his childlike faith could not wait. He had to have it now.

My first reaction was to persuade him to wait until we returned to America. Baptism is conducted in the local rivers of India, and those rivers are anything but hygienic. Carabaos are bathed there and cooled in the heat of the tropical day. The local laundry is done there. And worst of all, much human waste goes directly into the rivers. I wasn't at all happy with the thought of my son being baptized in that kind of water.

Matthew, however, could not be deflected from his goal. He was convinced that God was speaking to him and so, reluctantly, I gave my consent, and Jerry baptized Matthew in a foul-smelling Indian river. I was greatly relieved when Matthew seemed to suffer no ill-effects from the experience. To the contrary, it proved, for him, to be a thoroughly positive encounter with God.

One of the most thrilling events of our second visit to India was meeting a small boy in an orphanage we had been financially supporting. The boy quickly became attached to us, and we discovered one day that he was sleeping on our doorstep to be near us. We invited him in and let him share a room with Matthew. That thrilled Matthew immensely. We remembered seeing the boy's face in photographs sent to us, but that face on a photograph had now become a real person to us.

Those six weeks in India passed all too quickly and, before we knew it, we were on our way back to the airport to depart for home. I was thinking over the highlights of the trip and trying to stretch out my legs as the car jolted along the arid, desert road. It had been a good trip, and God had done many wonderful things. Matthew hadn't died from some tropical disease, after all. In fact, he had been confirmed in his faith. I smiled at the thought. I was so proud of him.

My happy reflections were rudely interrupted by a strange spluttering sound. The car ground to a halt, and silence enveloped us.

"What's happened?" Matthew asked anxiously.

"I'll go and look," our driver replied opening the door. Euphoria swiftly evaporated as we waited for a verdict. We were miles from any gas station or garage or help of any kind, and the thought of missing our plane raised such a complicated range of emotions that I promptly shut it out of my mind.

"Lord, don't let this be serious. Help us, please," I silently prayed.

The driver emerged from under the hood of the car, wiping his greasy hands on a rag. "The hose has gone," he announced gloomily.

The heat had deteriorated the hose leading from the fuel tank and now the fuel could no longer get to the engine. We were stranded.

Now that we were not moving, the heat was suffocating, and we squirmed with discomfort as our thin clothes clung to our bodies and moisture trickled down our faces. We all got out, but the heat outside was nearly as bad as it was inside. I suddenly remembered I had some foil-wrapped "freshen-up" Handiwipe tissues in my pocket, and I handed these out to everyone. The cool fragrance brought a few seconds of relief.

While our driver tried to figure out how to fix the faulty hose, Jerry got out, wandered a few feet away, and sat on a flat rock under a tree. I tried, somewhat unsuccessfully, to keep Matthew occupied while, at the same time, I was wondering how we were going to get to the airport on time.

Suddenly, Jerry leapt up from his rock yelling, "I've got it!"

He went over to the driver with the foil packet which had contained the moist tissue and, in great excitement, began to explain the solution to our problem.

"Look, this is what we are going to do. See this packet?

We're going to use it to cover the holes in the hose. How about that?"

The driver paused for a moment, obviously wondering if the hot sun had robbed Jerry of his reason; then he replied abruptly, "It won't work."

"What do you mean, it won't work? It will work. God told me it will work, so let's do it."

"Pastor," the man said firmly and quietly, as if pacifying a person of deranged mind, "It simply will not work."

"I'm telling you that it will work," Jerry insisted, "so we need to get on with it." He was obviously convinced that this bizarre idea would do the trick. I must admit I had a certain amount of sympathy for the driver. Knowing my husband's lack of mechanical prowess, it was certainly hard not to be sceptical about the feasibility of his proposal.

Jerry told me later that, as he sat on the rock crying out to God for help, he had heard the Lord say three times: "What is that in your hand?" Finally he had realized that the little foil packet he was nervously folding and unfolding with his fingers was the key to our dilemma.

In the absence of any better suggestion, the driver agreed to try Jerry's idea. He got in the first-aid box, took out a Band-Aid and attempted to fasten the foil packet to the hose with the Band-Aid. When he had everything in place, he slammed down the hood; we all scrambled to resume our seats; the engine roared to life and our spirits soared to the sky. Then there was a familiar cough and splutter, and we were back to square one. I thought the driver showed remarkable restraint not to yell, "I told you so."

The Band-Aid strip had, predictably, taken all of two seconds to curl up and fall from its position like an autumn leaf. "Perhaps we need something like wire to secure it," I remarked tentatively, realizing even as I spoke that this was probably not the most helpful contribution I could make to the situation. The nearest roll of wire was probably as inaccessible as everything else we needed right now.

"Lord, we need some wire to make this work. Please help us," Jerry prayed, and then he began marching off into the desert, presumably in search of more inspiration.

"Be careful," I yelled after his retreating figure.

"What's going to happen, Mom?" Matthew asked nervously.

"I have no idea, Matthew, but I'm sure the Lord is going to rescue us somehow," I reassured him with more conviction than I felt.

A few minutes later I saw my husband galloping at top speed toward the car. Considering the heat this was no mean feat. "What about this?" he announced triumphantly, if a trifle breathlessly. In his hand was a tiny coil of brand new wire.

"Wow, Dad, where did you find that?" Matthew asked.

"Just lying on the ground waiting for us," Jerry replied. "Thank you Lord!"

I supplied another foil packet, the wire was attached, and once again we took a deep breath as the engine turned over and the car began to move forward. Being somewhat faithless, I expected it to shudder to a halt any moment. However, we travelled for many miles over uneven roads with nothing but a foil packet and a piece of wire to keep the holes in that hose covered. God enabled us to arrive at the airport in time to catch our plane home.

For some time after that I carried one of those foil packets around with me everywhere I went and told many people the story. The method we used might not work for others, and it might not work for us again. It worked that day because God allowed it to work to rescue us from a serious predicament.

On the way home, Jerry told us later that as he had walked out into the desert praying for some wire, he had remembered a story told by David "Little David" Walker at Bible college. As a child he was out one day with his father who was an evangelist. Miles from anywhere they had a flat tire. They also had no spare. Little David described how his father walked off into the countryside praying. He came back sometime later rolling a tire he had found. It was exactly the type they required for the car they were driving.

When he remembered this story, Jerry had said to the Lord, "Father, I don't need a tire, but I do need some wire. Please help me. Your Word says that You do not show partiality. You did it for Little David's father, and I know that You can do it for me today." It wasn't long afterward that he spied the coil of wire lying there as if it had been dropped from Heaven.

We were on our way home again.

Chapter Seventeen

Strange Singing In the Night

Another of God's graces has been demonstrated powerfully in our lives, His power to heal our sicknesses. One event stands out clearly in my mind.

The room was dark, and I lay still in bed, praying that the terrible pounding pain in my head would diminish. We had been away for the weekend with a team from the Bible college where we were now teaching. I did not exactly feel at the peak of physical fitness when we set out, for we had been working very hard. Our lives were immersed in the college and Christian school and also in raising our family. After several hours of travelling we had embarked on a series of meetings.

"Gail, you're going to have to speak at the meeting tonight," Jerry announced hoarsely, his usually powerful voice reduced to a rasping croak. He had managed to contract laryngitis.

I was totally unprepared and, what is worse, I had come away in such a rush that I had forgotten my Bible. I borrowed my sister's Bible, but the layout of it was different, and I had a hard time quickly finding what I needed. The Lord showed me quite clearly that I should speak about the experiences of Job when he endured unspeakable pain, yet ultimately emerged triumphant from his personal crucible of suffering. If I had only known that I was preaching to myself.

Now I felt a new sympathy with the boil-covered Job as I struggled with the pain in my head which was gradually becoming more intense. We had arrived home in the early hours of the morning, and I wasn't feeling well. When I was unable to lift my head from the pillow the next morning, Jerry thought I had just overextended myself and left me to sleep longer. When he returned later that day to check on my progress, however, his forehead was furrowed with anxiety.

"Gail, honey, I think we had better get you to the doctor," he said gently.

"No, I'll be okay. I just need to sleep it off," I replied.

But I could not sleep it off, and soon I was lying in a hospital bed at the beginning of a nightmare of helplessness that would last for many months.

After tests had been done, doctors informed Jerry that I had an aneurism of the brain, and that I was in a very life-threatening condition. I was transferred to another hospital, and my condition quickly deteriorated to the point that I was unable to recognize my husband or children. My life hung in the balance, and my family was told that if the aneurism ruptured, I could be dead in seconds. Eventually, it did rupture, but I survived, which certainly gave the medical experts food for thought.

Helpless, I lay in a neuro-intensive care unit. The prognosis was that if I lived I would probably be in a vegetative state the rest of my life — if I lived.

During this difficult period, something wonderful happened. I had forgotten my husband. I had forgotten my children. I had even forgotten my own name. Oddly enough, however, I had not forgotten God's Word. As I lay there in the hospital, it seemed as if a tape recorder was playing inside my head:

> *[Jesus] is a friend that sticketh closer than a brother.*
> Proverbs 18:24

> *I am the Lord that healeth thee.*   Exodus 15:26

Many other such promises went through my head in those moments. I believe that as people prayed, the Lord was beginning to heal me from the inside out.

One night the excruciating pain returned to my head, and I cried out to God in utter torment and agony. Suddenly the room was filled with the most beautiful singing I have ever heard. Someone was singing that old favorite hymn of the Church: "'Tis so sweet to trust in Jesus, just take Him at His Word." It sounded to me like the voice of a black lady singing and, as she sang, the pain began to decrease.

She not only sang, she quoted the Scripture, and she preached. I wasn't quite sure if I was imagining all this, or whether I was hallucinating or poised at the gateway of Heaven having a preview of angelic worship. I called out, "Nurse, is someone singing?"

"I'm sorry," the nurse replied. "Is it bothering you?"

"No," I managed to answer. "I just wanted to know what was happening."

"I'm afraid I can't stop her," she said. "She is unconscious. I don't want you to be disturbed though."

"I'm fine. Don't worry about it," I replied. "It's beautiful."

During that night, as an unconscious woman ministered God's Word to me, I was being healed. God's ways are truly amazing!

Doctors had told Jerry that I would never again be able to perform even simple tasks like sweeping the floor and that climbing steps could kill me. Yet, by the power of God, I was restored to lead a completely full and normal life. Jesus has promised to be with us through our storms and sicknesses, and this is the transforming factor that makes triumph possible.

Daniel had to face his lion's den, and his three Hebrew friends had to face their fiery furnace, but God was with them. Job was a righteous man, yet he suffered as part of God's plan. At one point, because of the misery of his physical situation, Job had lost sight of God, but in the end he was able to say:

He knoweth the way that I take: when he hath tried me, I shall come forth as gold.   Job 23:10

The end of Job's life was more blessed than the beginning, and that is saying something. At the beginning he was wealthy and successful and had everything that the natural man could desire. By the end of the book, however, he not only had all that, but he also had a depth of relationship with God which he could have only dreamed of before.

God's promise to us is:

The people who do know their God shall be strong and do exploits.   Daniel 11:32

May all the glory and honor be unto our Lord Jesus, our great Healer, our great Provider, our great Deliverer!

CHAPTER EIGHTEEN

FULL HOUSE - EMPTY FIELDS

We had become very settled in our comfortable American lifestyle. Matthew was now sixteen, and our twin daughters were twelve, and it seemed right to consider their future needs. We had just completed a beautiful custom-built house for ourselves, but we had also invested in some apartments with the idea that the income from them would finance our children's future education.

God was blessing us. Jerry was administrative dean of the Bible college and principal of a Christian academy attached to the church. I was an administrator, counsellor, teacher and ran a children's church. Life was good.

But just at this point when we began to think about retirement and security, God began to stir us, beckoning us towards a new challenge in our lives. As often happens, the exact nature of that change was still concealed from us.

We became aware first that we needed to resign our positions in the local church before God showed us the next step in His plans for us. Somewhat reluctantly and with questions in our minds about timing, we went to talk it over with the pastor of the church. He listened carefully to what we had to say and then asked, "Where do you feel God is calling you to go?"

"We have no idea," Jerry replied. "We just know that it's time to move on."

There was a silence and the pastor's brow registered anxiety. The lines on his pale skin settled into a frown as he digested this obviously unwelcome news. Finally, he spoke: "I have no one to take your place in the college. What about the children's work and all the training programs you are running? Would you consider staying at least until you have a clearer idea of where God wants you to go? This would at least give me time to look for replacements."

His suggestion seemed like a perfectly reasonable idea at the time, and we agreed to stay in our positions until our future course of action was revealed. In retrospect we realized we would have saved ourselves a considerable amount of anguish and heartache if we had acted on the Lord's original words and resigned there and then. Up until this time things had been running very smoothly. The academy had a waiting list and the college was thriving. We were happy in our work, accepted by those we worked with and fulfilled. The next school year was to prove the most devastating time in our whole ministry. We had let our natural minds take over and reason things out in a logical way, and when anyone lets that happen, he or she is about to miss God's best. A very difficult situation was soon to develop which would make us wish we had obeyed.

I learned of the problem one day as I entered the girls rest room. A group of girls stood clustered tightly together in one corner talking. They were so engrossed in the subject of their whispered conversation that they didn't hear me come in. I thought I caught the word *preg-*

nant before one of them half-turned and silenced the others who all exchanged guilty looks.

"Who's pregnant?" I asked quietly.

A tense silence filled the room. The girls studied their shoes or focused their eyes on a distant wash basin. I waited, and the atmosphere became more and more tense. The suspense was finally ended as one of the girls blurted out a name. The girl they had heard was pregnant turned out to be someone greatly respected by the young people in the church.

"Is it true, Mrs. Rozell?" they asked, shocked and worried by this news.

I didn't know. The church leaders had apparently decided to keep this situation from us for as long as possible. The parents of the boy concerned were prominent church members of the church and, although the school was well known for its strong stand on moral issues, the leaders had apparently believed that they might lose a significant amount of financial support if this matter became public knowledge.

When we went to the authorities about this matter, we felt we had no alternative but to speak out and make our position clear: "These two young people have done something wrong, and we cannot cover it up and pretend it has not happened. Yes, we must love them and help them in every way possible but, at the end of the day, sin is sin. It needs to be called sin and dealt with as sin. We believe that the only right way forward is to ask them both to leave the academy."

Voices were immediately raised in angry dissent: "Oh come on, that is a bit drastic, isn't it?"

"Yes," another voice chimed in. "This is a crucial time

in their education. We can still discipline them without going that far, can't we?"

"But what sort of signal will that send to other students?" I asked.

"That we stand for Christian love and forgiveness, I would hope," someone answered. "We all make mistakes. What about the command *'Judge not'*?"

We felt that to compromise on this point would send a very wrong signal to the other students, but the other leaders did not agree, and we were overruled. The students were allowed to stay.

After this happened, we felt ostracized, classified as hard-hearted villains for recommending a harsh, unreasonable sentence on two young people who, after all, were hardly more than children. But the moral question was far more important to us. As we saw it, we had two options. We could condone what had happened and stay, or object to the ruling and quit. We chose the latter, so, with heavy hearts, we handed in our letters of resignation after seven years of service to the church and school. In order not to cause confusion among the members of the church, we agreed to finish what was left of the school year and not to tell anyone about our decision and why we were leaving.

It was not quite that easy. Some of the members came to know what was happening and urged us to start another church, but this we would not do. Nevertheless, many accusations were made against us by the leadership of the church and there followed a very lonely and painful time in our Christian experience. We kept a low profile for a time, but many tears were shed in the privacy of our home as we tried to deal with hurts and disappointments that we could not understand and probably never will.

I was so hurt by the way we had been treated that I did a foolish thing. I decided that, since I had never been treated in this way in the world, I would just leave the ministry and go back to secular work. I had sold some real estate to help support our family and still had my license, so I decided that when my obligations were fulfilled with the school, I would start selling again. Maybe then I could put this whole affair behind me. Jerry felt the same way and decided that he would also seek a secular position.

In the meantime, we were again struggling financially. Our salaries had been quite small anyway and when we resigned, they ended, leaving us short of cash for daily living. One day we returned home from a preaching engagement and all I had left was a little minced meat to feed the family. As a mother I was deeply troubled by the fact that I could not provide a proper meal for my husband and children. As we walked towards the front door, our neighbor, a Christian from another church, called out to me, "Gail, I have something for you."

I walked across the lawn to meet her, and she handed me some potatoes and other vegetables. "These are the firstfruits of our garden," she said. "I hope you won't be insulted, but you are people of God, and I wanted to give them to you."

I thanked her profusely and walked indoors, uplifted by the knowledge that God had not deserted us, and His provision for our family never failed during this difficult time.

We continued to run firmly on course to leave the

ministry, but one day God sent an evangelist to our church, and his coming changed the direction of our lives forever. A visitor would have had no reason to suspect anything was wrong in our lives just then. We continued to teach, lead worship and preach in the local church and appeared to be totally involved in the life of the Christian community. Inwardly, however, we were dead and were just ticking off the days until our liberation would come.

I had never seen this particular evangelist before and, as far as I know, I have never seen him since. I still can't remember his name or anything about the way he looked. What I do remember is that he preached a message that halted us in our tracks and kept us from forsaking God's will for our lives.

At the time, I was in another part of the church building working with the children's church. There was a buzz of activity as the children worked on a project, and I decided to slip into the back of the church and listen to the visitor for a few minutes. As I entered, the man was just rising to speak. His voice seemed to fill every corner of the building. "What are you asking God for?" he thundered. "Are you asking Him for a new home? Are you asking Him for success in real estate? Are you asking for a Lincoln Continental?" He paused and then declared emphatically, "All these things are trash."

I shifted on my chair uncomfortably, unable to believe my ears. We had built a new home. I was about to return to a career in real estate, and I was driving a Lincoln Continental. Yet this man was telling me that these things were all *trash* in God's eyes. He read from the Psalms:

A Reed In His Right Hand

Ask of me and I will make the nations your inherit-
ance and the ends of the earth your possession.

Psalm 2:8, NIV

"God wants to give us nations," he said. "He wants us to ask Him for the heathen. If we ask, He will give them to us."

Suddenly and uncontrollably, tears began to flow, as the Holy Spirit began to expose how wrong my perspective on life had become. He began to whisper urgently into my heart: "Never mind all that is going on. Never mind what people are saying. Never mind all the pain and anguish in your life at the moment. Ask Me for souls."

I thought of D. L. Moody's famous prayer: "Give me souls lest I die."

At that moment I was consumed by a passion for God to give me men and women who would come to know Him. I felt that nothing else mattered, and that if only God would grant me that desire, I would be satisfied.

I had to get up and return to the children, although the rest of that morning my mind was distracted by the pleading voice of God: "Ask Me for souls. Ask Me for the nations."

When we left for home that day, Jerry said, "You should have heard the message today."

"I did hear it," I said, "but I don't want to talk about it." For the moment, I found it impossible to articulate the mix of feelings I was experiencing.

This was not an unusual response on my part. Sometimes, when God is dealing deeply with me, I find myself immersed in a cocoon of silence, as I struggle to come to terms with what He is saying. Sometimes I am just overwhelmed by His closeness and all this makes communication immensely difficult.

For a long time after this I kept hearing those words repeated over and over again somewhere deep inside my being: "Ask Me for souls. Ask Me for the nations." It was a powerful and insistent message from which there was no escape. I would wake in the night to find them racing around in my mind, and as I awoke in the morning they would still be there, compelling me to respond to the pleas of a God who did not want even one of His creatures to perish.

At about this time God also began to remind me of an old song that I had not heard for years. Suddenly it seemed to be everywhere. If I turned on the radio it was there, or if I went to church it would be sung:

> *"My house is full, but My fields are empty.*
> *Who will go and work for Me today?"*

The words were as poignant and persuasive as the words of the psalm the evangelist had used.

God was also using the song and the psalm to speak to Jerry. We had wanted to give up, but the reality of God's Word was making an impact on our lives. It was bringing new strength and purpose to us. The Bible was making clear to us once again that everything, even Heaven and Earth, would someday come to an end, and that only what was done for Christ would last.

Chapter Nineteen

Where Is Zimbabwe?

Another visiting speaker who impacted our lives was Pastor Ron Kinnear from South Africa. He had come to our church to talk about the needs in Africa and about his work in a Bible college in Zimbabwe. We were blessed to have him visit our home one evening.

That night he said to Jerry and me in his quaint South African accent, "You are just the kind of people we need in Zimbabwe. You have the right kind of background and a wide variety of experience in life." He continued, stroking his neat beard, "It is too bad that you are so committed here. We could use you in Zimbabwe."

I gave Jerry a meaningful glance, but we both remained silent. Doubts about the wisdom of this invitation began to fill my mind as I tried not to catch the eye of this dapper little man whose words made me feel uncomfortable. We had still not fully emerged from our pit of despair. Surely it was too early to begin thinking about some major change in our lives.

But something had stirred in us when we heard Ron speaking in church. We still had a great interest in missions, and normally we would have been the first to invite a visiting missionary to our home, but were actually reluctant at first to ask Ron to spend time with us. Deep wounds had not yet healed, and we didn't want to be drawn into conversations which were difficult for us. It was easier to keep everyone at arm's length for now.

At last the evening came to an end. As he rose to go, Pastor Kinnear said, "I'm going to be travelling to a number of places. I'll leave you a copy of my itinerary and then you will be able to contact me if you want to for any reason."

We accepted the itinerary, smiled politely and, with relief, ushered our guest to the front door. In spite of all that God had been saying to us, our position regarding our future had not changed. We had not the slightest intention of going to Africa. We were committed to leaving the Christian ministry and were waiting to scuttle back to the relative safety of "ordinary employment."

But God had not finished with us yet. One morning Jerry said to me with unaccustomed vehemence, "I hate that song. I hate that song."

"What song?" I asked.

"My house is full, and My fields are empty," he replied grimly. "All night that song has been going round and round in my mind. I hate it."

Later that day I was idly flicking through the television channels, looking for something to watch, when a small boy came on the screen. I can remember registering surprise as it was a channel we could not normally receive. Then I suddenly heard the boy's words, "Mommy, where is Zimbabwe?"

From this point on not only did we keep running into the song and the psalm, but we were also pursued by constant references to the country of Zimbabwe. It was very strange.

Like the boy on the television, I did not even know where Zimbabwe was situated. It had only recently gained independence, and I would only have recognized it under the old name of Southern Rhodesia.

God continued to deal with us until we could no longer ignore what He was saying. Eventually we agreed to go to Zimbabwe for six weeks. We felt that we could not stay longer. We would do as much as we could during that time, but we stated categorically that we would not be staying indefinitely. So we began to make preparations to leave for Africa.

When we were finally on the plane to Africa, I can remember turning over in my mind all the events of the past few months and wondering what it all meant. Then the sweet Spirit of God spoke to my heart and said, "They meant it for evil, but I meant it for good."

Soon the wheels bumped down on the tarmac, and I saw the words "Welcome to Zimbabwe" on the airport building in Harare. I hadn't noticed that I was weeping. God was changing my heart.

Chapter Twenty

What's Wrong?

During the next six weeks in Zimbabwe, we taught in the Bible college and ministered in many parts of the country. The highlight of the trip was a conference at a place called Rufaro. About five thousand Africans gathered there in a very primitive setting with no running water or electricity, a world far removed from our Western lifestyle.

The building in which we were housed was teeming with rats. Hot water was obtainable only by heating a pan on the old wood stove in the kitchen. And there were many other lacks. But I can honestly say all these things ceased to be significant to me when I witnessed the hunger of the people for God's Word. The evidence of God's power at work in this humble situation touched us very deeply.

One evening we were sitting in our temporary home looking out at a velvety black sky. It was pierced by myriads of sparkling silver pinheads. We could hear the crackling of camp fires and the murmur of voices like the droning of many deep-voiced insects, as people settled down for another night in the open air. A dog barked, and there was the rustling of leaves in a stand of trees behind the hut. I felt relaxed and peaceful.

Noticing a tape recorder on a shelf, I switched it on and pressed the "play" button. A melody drifted through the room and out into the beauty of the African night. It was a song we had come to know only too well:

"My house is full, and My fields are empty.
Who will go and work for Me today?"

Tears flowed unchecked as we sat there, so far away from home and yet still relentlessly pursued by this haunting song. Jerry turned off the tape recorder and sat down again.

"What's wrong," Pastor Kinnear asked, looking concerned.

There was a long silence and then, taking a deep breath, Jerry blurted out: "It's that song. I can't take any more of it. I can't take that song."

"What do you mean, Jerry?" the pastor inquired gently.

We proceeded to pour out to him how this song had followed us around the world and we could not seem to escape it. Now the eyes of the pastor became moist, and soon he was weeping openly as he described to us his visit to America.

"As I was travelling around sharing my vision for Zimbabwe, it seemed that no one was interested. Nobody seemed to have a burden from God for this country. Every night I would go to my room and play that same song you have been talking about. I would cry out to God, pleading with Him to make somebody care about Zimbabwe. 'Please speak to someone, Lord,' I pleaded, 'and tell them to come and help us.' "

The whole thing suddenly struck me as funny and I

began to accuse the pastor of planting his tape recorder in our bedroom so that we would keep hearing the song. We still joke about it today, but God began to complete another phase in His dealings with us while we were there in Africa on that six-week trip.

He spoke to Jerry first and told him that he would return to the Living Waters Bible College and assist Pastor Kinnear. We were both, in fact, invited to take up teaching positions at the college.

Then one day I was standing by a pool when God spoke to me and made it clear that the Kinnears would not be at the college much longer. We were to return and work there. It seemed extremely unlikely that the Kinnears would be leaving Living Waters, but I stored the thought away in my mind.

The six weeks ended, and we returned home promising God that if He supplied the finances and opened the way for us to return to Zimbabwe, we would gladly obey.

CHAPTER TWENTY-ONE

A MAJOR CAREER CHANGE

Once more on home turf, our first move was to call a family conference. We had taught our children that it was important to pray together as a family and to seek God's direction together. Now we told them, in the simplest way possible, that we believed God wanted us to go to Africa. Three shocked faces stared back at us in disbelief.

Our children were accustomed to the comforts of American life, and somehow they sensed that the unknown Africa would present some challenges which they did not altogether relish. Questions rained thick and fast, but before it was over, everyone agreed to pray about it. When their response did come, it moved us deeply. "If that is what God is saying," they told us, "then there is nothing else that we can do but go." We praised God that our children were prepared to react in this way and preparations began in earnest for a move to Zimbabwe.

The United States was undergoing a recession at the time, and the real estate market was sluggish as a result. But we were able to sell our apartments. I found it hard to cut all our strings to home, so we kept our house for another year. It represented a security blanket, an escape route in case things did not work out for us in Africa.

A Major Career Change

Many people, moved by our testimony in the churches, promised to support us as missionaries on the field, so on July 7, 1982, we set off to start a new life.

It seemed, however, that most of those people who had promised their financial support, forgot their promises. Only a few months after we arrived in Zimbabwe things were so bad financially that Jerry went out one night, looked up into the sky, and cried out to God: "God, You have said in Your Word that You will not let the righteous be forsaken or his seed have to beg bread. We can go back to America and work, but if we are righteous and have Your call, You can make a way." This was hardly the grand beginning we had imagined for our ministry in Zimbabwe.

The five of us were living with the Kinnears and their three children in a three-bedroom house. The Kinnears were very gracious, but two families wedged into a confined space is never an easy situation.

The other problem was that, on the very day we arrived at their house, they told us they would shortly be leaving the country (just as God had told me during our previous trip) and that they would be giving up their house.

So here we were, in a foreign country, with no money, nowhere to live and the people we had come to assist were about to leave town. It was certainly a test of faith. We had nowhere else to turn except to our faithful God, and that is what Jerry did.

"How much money do we have?" Jerry asked me as he came back inside.

"We have only about a hundred dollars left," I answered.

"We're going to give that money to the college," he told me.

"Give it away?" I was incredulous. "And what are we supposed to do then?"

"We're going to trust God, and if He does not meet our needs, then we will find a way to get back home."

We gave the money to the college, without anyone knowing that it was all we had left.

A few days later we went to the post office to collect our mail. There was an envelope waiting for us with an unfamiliar name and address in Oklahoma. This was intriguing as we had never been to Oklahoma, and could not remember having any contacts there.

We ripped open the envelope and discovered a check for three thousand dollars inside. We looked in the envelope again, but there was no note of explanation. We were totally overwhelmed by what God had done for us.

There was a return address on the envelope, so we mailed a letter as quickly as possible, thanking the people in Oklahoma for their generosity and explaining how God had used it to bail us out of a difficult situation. This was the reply we received:

"I am a student at Oral Roberts University. One day I was sitting in a classroom studying missions and, in particular, giving to missions. God spoke to me very clearly and told me that He wanted me to give three thousand dollars to a missionary who was in a desperate situation. I was puzzled because I didn't even know a missionary. When I opened my Bible, I found your prayer-prompter bookmark which a friend in North Carolina had given to me. God said, 'That is the missionary. I want you to send the money now.' "

A Major Career Change

We were temporarily speechless as we contemplated the fact that in our moment of crisis God had bypassed all the expected channels of support and had selected an unknown, a student in Oklahoma. He had then guided into the hands of that student a bookmark that was used to answer our prayer. What God won't do for those who love Him! We felt much better now about our beginning in Zimbabwe.

One day before we had left home, we had been talking to Jerry's mom, when she handed him a magazine article. "If you are going to Zimbabwe, this might be of interest to you," she said. It was entitled "The Ostrich People," and described an unusual tribe in Zimbabwe with a genetic deformity which resulted in two-toed feet. The structure of the foot bore a distinct resemblance to that of the ostrich, hence the name *Ostrich People*. "Who knows, you might come across them," she added smiling.

As Jerry read the article, God spoke into his heart in a very powerful and unexpected way: "I am going to use you to bring the good news of My Son to these people."

The words were clear and unmistakable, leaving an indelible imprint on his mind so that he knew he would never forget them. Jerry was so overwhelmed by the reality of God's presence that day that tears came to his eyes.

As we drove away from his parents' home that day I marvelled again at all the events which had led us to this point of time. Going to Zimbabwe would have seemed totally unbelievable only a few months earlier, let alone the possibility of encountering a tribe of two-toed people who had never heard the Gospel.

Despite the pressures of the opportunities before us,

thoughts of "The Ostrich People" were never far from our minds. Jerry had shared the vision with a fellow missionary named Doug Sandison, a graduate of Christ for the Nations Institute in Dallas, Texas. We knew now that we had to wait for the right moment to move forward on this vision.

Meanwhile, I had another problem. It was November and our first college graduation day in Zimbabwe. The house was overflowing with various guest pastors and other visitors. Caught up in the whirl of cooking and serving, I became aware of a nagging pain in my side which could not be ignored. I told myself that there was no time at the moment to think about aches, but smiling, talking cheerfully, and trying to anticipate the needs of my guests became more and more difficult. In the kitchen, I clutched a cupboard as a wave of unbearable pain caused me to catch my breath sharply. I gritted my teeth and managed to carry on until Jerry and the guests left for a meeting at the college.

Trying desperately to ignore what was happening, I took a visiting missionary to visit one of my friends. Before long, however, I had to recognize that something serious was wrong with me. The pain was becoming more and more acute, and I did not know what to do with myself. I asked someone to take me home. Hoping that lying down would help, I went to bed, but soon I found myself rushing to the toilet to vomit, and, at this point, I was nearly screaming from the pain. An hour later I was in a hospital.

A nightmare blur of events followed, interspersed with panic, prayer and pain. I remember a filthy and chaotic emergency room full of noise and people and a seemingly half-blind, white lady doctor who looked as

A Major Career Change

if she had been hauled out of retirement and who certainly had long ago abandoned such sentimental trivia
as a sympathetic bedside manner.

I was given X-rays and more X-rays.

"We think it is a kidney stone," she finally told me, as
she gave me an injection.

Jerry's face was, to me, an oasis of love and concern
in a cold, uncaring wilderness of churlish indifference.
He was looking at me as I drifted off to sleep.

I woke up, however, feeling alone, bewildered and
very, very sick. Jerry had gone home. As I struggled to
get out of bed, pain hit my body with the ferocity of a
frenzied knife attack. I managed to stop myself from
sinking to the floor and, stooping forward and clutch-
ing my stomach, I got into the hall. Through a shimmering haze, I saw a group of nurses talking and laughing,
as if they were enjoying a lazy evening's leisure at a pave-
ment cafe.

"Excuse me," I whispered. "Please, can you tell me
where the toilet is?" They seemed offended by the in-
trusion, but one of them finally told me, in a decidedly
offhand manner, that there was a bathroom in my room.
Fighting back tears, I weakly tried to push open the
heavy door. No one came to my aid.

What makes human beings so callous, I wondered, *that
they can hardly manage to be civil when faced with the vul-
nerability of the suffering?* I would have given anything
that night for a little tenderness and concern.

When a diagnosis was finally reached, I was told, "It's
not a stone, but it appears you may need surgery."

Days passed before anyone could tell me more about
what was wrong with me. Furthermore, no one seemed
to care whether I lived or died. When Jerry tried to get a

specialist, he was told that because we were "only missionaries" it was impossible. Under the socialist rules of the new regime, we had to take whatever doctor was available.

After several weeks of sickness, we were finally able to secure the services of a good doctor, and he discovered that I had a twisted bowel and that gangrene had already set in. Eventually I was operated on — when it was nearly too late.

My recovery was slow. After three weeks had passed, I was still lying helpless in a hospital bed. I had been vomiting continuously for three weeks, and I felt that I was getting weaker and weaker. It was nearly Christmas, but even the effort of thinking involved too much energy. My prayers even seemed feeble: "Oh God, I'm never going to make it out of here, am I?"

I thought of the children. It was their first Christmas away from home. Tears blurred my eyes. They needed me. What was I doing here creeping ever closer to death in this hospital ward? Despair swamped me.

Looking up, I saw the large, familiar figure of one of the young white elders from the church approaching the bed. "Gail, I would like to give you communion," he said.

"I would love to have it," I whispered weakly, "but I don't think I could keep it down. Everything that passes my lips makes me sick."

"I'm so sorry," he answered.

At that moment I believe that God spoke to me. He said, "My body was broken and My blood was shed that you might live. If you will eat of My body today and if you drink of My blood today, then you will live."

Somehow I took hold of those words and said to the

elder, "Sorry, I want to try. Please will you give me a very small piece of bread."

He passed me a crumb and I put it into my mouth. A tremendous struggle ensued as I tried desperately hard not to vomit. I took a sip of the cup and cried out to God from the depths of my being, "God, You promised me that Your body was broken and Your blood was shed that I might live."

From the moment that I took hold of those words in my spirit, strength began to come back into my body, and within three days I was home with my family. It took some more time to recover fully, but I was eating and walking again, and I was with my children and husband for Christmas.

Not long after I recovered from that surgery, our lives were miraculously spared again — this time from a traffic accident. The van had been full of joking and laughter as we drove down the street together. It was New Year's Day, and we were returning from watching Matthew play in a baseball match. It was so good to be with the family again. We had so enjoyed ourselves together.

Suddenly there was an alarming high-pitched squeal of rubber tires, followed by a loud, grinding thud, and then the world went mad.

I could feel myself being thrown about as the van turned over. Someone screamed, and I was conscious of raising my hands to shield my face as I hurtled toward the windshield. Just as my head should have struck it, it burst outward, showering glass over the road. Before it was over, we rolled over three times and landed upside down.

"Are you alright?" everyone asked at once.

"Yes," came the answer, again in unison.

"Are you okay, Mom?" the children asked.

"Yes, I'm fine," I said. "What about you?"

Everyone seemed to be fine, and shaking, we helped each other out of the smashed vehicle.

It seemed that a car had failed to stop at a stop sign and had hit us broadside. Glass was everywhere. Practically every window was broken and glass was spewed all over the road. No one would ever ride in that van again, and the other car was seriously damaged, as well, but not one of us was seriously injured. How we thanked God for sparing our lives once again!

Everyone was greatly concerned for me because I had only recently come home from the hospital after major surgery. They took me to be examined, and the surgeon who looked me over was amazed to discover that I was completely intact.

I had bruises on many parts of my body, but the place of the incision had been totally protected. "If you had hit the wound," the doctor said, "it would have burst open, and you would probably have died." That certainly didn't leave anything to the imagination.

It was only later that I realized what was happening during those early months, the financial lack, my surgery, the accident. God had entrusted to us a mission of great importance; He had promised to use us to bring the Gospel to a tribe who had never heard of Jesus, and Satan was not about to let that work go forward unhindered. With God's help, we were determined to go forward.

CHAPTER TWENTY-TWO

IN SEARCH OF THE OSTRICH PEOPLE

In January of 1983, Jerry became principal of the Living Waters Bible College, and there were, as a result, many new claims on his time. He could not, however, forget the words of the Holy Spirit regarding the Vadoma tribe, or the Ostrich People as many called them. A burden for those people still burned in his heart.

Soon after we had arrived in Zimbabwe, we began to make inquiries about the tribe and were slightly disconcerted to discover that no one seemed to have heard of them. We asked a leading African pastor what he knew about this tribe. He smiled in a wry, knowing kind of way and said: "I think someone is trying to tease you. There are no such people in Zimbabwe. I have lived here all my life, and I have never heard of them."

"But God has told me that He wants me to share the Gospel with them," Jerry protested.

"Well," the pastor replied, shaking his head, "if God told you, then they must be here somewhere. All I can say is that I have never heard of them."

Jerry eventually decided to take his investigation to the Zimbabwean government, and eventually was able to secure an appointment with an official at the Ministry of Rural Planning and Development in Harare.

"Before I came to Zimbabwe," he began his explanation, "I read about the Vadoma people, but since arriving here I have not been able to locate anyone who can confirm their existence. I am hoping that you will be able to help me."

The black, smartly suited official sat rigidly behind his huge desk, which was covered by piles of forms and a variety of rubber stamps. Without a trace of a smile on his face he replied, "Yes, the Vadoma exist, but they don't need you to bring them religion."

"Sir," Jerry replied, "I have no intention of bringing them religion. I just want to bring them Christ. Please, will you tell me where they live and what language they speak."

Pointing to a large map which filled the wall behind the desk, the man told Jerry that if he travelled due east of Harare he would find the Vadoma tribe near the Mozambique border. He added that their native tongue was Tonga. Jerry thanked him and almost danced out of the room, extremely excited by what he had discovered. As he climbed into his vehicle, however, he felt a tremendous sense of hesitation. He sat there for a moment in deep thought and then heard the warning voice of God's Spirit: "This man has lied to you. You will not find the Vadoma people in the place he told you to look."

We were all thrilled to hear that at last someone had confirmed the existence of this strange tribe, but we were also discouraged that we had made no progress at all in discovering their whereabouts. Convinced that Jerry's feeling that the official had lied was well founded, we spread out a huge map of Zimbabwe on the floor of the lounge and began to pray: "Lord, we've tried everything to find the Ostrich People. We tried the Christian pastors; we tried the government; but no one seems willing or able to help us find these people. Lord, You told us so clearly that You wanted us to share the Gospel with the Ostrich People. Please show us where to go."

Before long Jerry felt that his attention was being directed to a place called Kanyemba due north of Harare, on the border with Zambia. After he told us what he felt God was saying, he called Doug Sandison and asked him to come over.

"Kanyemba?" Doug said. "Yes, I know it like the back of my hand. I spent several months in the area when I was in the army. It's real bush country up there."

"What about the Ostrich People? Did you ever see anyone from this tribe?" Jerry asked, leaning forward eagerly.

"Sorry Jerry, not a sign of them, I'm afraid. You know, I had never heard of them until you mentioned the name."

We all sat back, somewhat deflated by this news, but we later decided that Kanyemba was the best place to start, and from that point made serious preparations for a trek out to that area.

Doug and his wife Mae wanted to be involved, and we also invited Patrick Musaka, a first year student at the college, to join the team. Patrick could speak the Tonga language.

Our first need was a sturdy vehicle that could traverse the dirt tracks in that primitive part of the country, and we began to ask God to supply something suitable. When Freda Lindsay and the folks at Christ For the Nations heard about our venture, they sent Doug six thousand dollars earmarked for reaching the Vadoma people, and with that money we bought a Land Rover.

A Reed In His Right Hand

The Land Rover was not exactly in peak condition. It was already twenty-five years old, but we believed it would suit our purpose. Then, we were able to purchase other necessary equipment for the expedition.

On Saturday, April 23, 1983, we stowed the last cot, camp stove and gas light in the ancient green Land Rover. At last, after many months of anticipation, we were ready to begin our journey in search of the Vadoma. The prospect of actually meeting this elusive tribe and bringing them the news of God's love filled us with indescribable elation.

We were not familiar with the Kanyemba area, and had only our faith that this was the place the Holy Spirit had indicated to Jerry. There were many dangers and uncertainties ahead, but we knew that God had given us a mission to undertake and, believing this was the right time, we committed ourselves into His hands.

I clambered into the vehicle, my heart bursting with excitement and my stomach knotted with fear, and we set off. It was 5:00 a.m.

The air was fresh and cool at that time of the morning and it caressed the surface of our skin. For the first three hours the roads were paved, but about thirty minutes beyond a town called Guruve we watched the road deteriorate into a dusty, rutted track. Now the endurance test began.

As its gears were shifted ever downward, the Land Rover was transformed from a docile beast to an aggressive rodeo stallion, violently bucking and rearing. I clung on, white-knuckled, as we were thrown mercilessly around the vehicle, until I felt as if every inch of my anatomy was being pounded into a pulp. It was unbearably hot, and rivulets of moisture trickled down my forehead, upper lip and the small of my back. I tried to fight the myriads of tiny flies that were swarming everywhere and settling all over us in their frantic quest for moisture. It was one of those times when thoughts stray from noble ideas and visions to grappling with overwhelming obsessions like how to arrange immediate total immersion in ice-cold water.

I longed for the ordeal to be over. The enthusiasm of our departure earlier that morning had rapidly faded. As if mirroring my own feelings, our fiery steed gave one last shudder and settled into silence.

"What on earth is that dreadful smell?" I inquired.

The air was filled with the sickening stench of something burning.

"We'd better take a look," Doug declared running his tanned fingers through his dark hair.

We all got out of the vehicle, and Mae and myself were put on wild-animal watch, while Jerry and Doug disappeared under the green hood to locate the source of the terrible smell. Patrick stood by, ready to give advice should that be required.

"There isn't much Doug can't fix," Mae told me confidently, her blonde hair shining brightly like filaments of gold in the strong light. I sincerely hoped that she was right. The ferocious heat of the Zambezi valley sun seemed to sap every vestige of energy from us, and we searched for some shade as the burning desert sand scorched our feet.

There was not a tree to be seen, only endless leafless bushes, a legacy of years of unrelenting drought. Not relishing falling victim to the long razor sharp thorns many of these bushes harbored, we decided to retire to the Land Rover for cover. After a great while, the hood was slammed down and the men joined us.

"The battery has exploded and covered the engine with acid," Doug diagnosed. "I'm afraid that there is nothing we can do but wait for another vehicle to pass."

We were stranded in a distinctly hostile wilderness far from tow trucks and gas stations. Days could pass before another vehicle came our way, and we had all heard our share of horror stories featuring the fate of stranded travellers. Walking was out of the question, and we knew that many "shumba" (lions) and other potentially dangerous animals roamed this area.

The heat was unbearable and the flies a total menace. We tried covering ourselves with nets but soon abandoned these as they severely restricted our ability to breathe. Bringing the situation to God, we tried to encourage each other, but deep down I guess we were all fearful. Time seemed to have stopped.

"Help, Jesus," was the cry of my heart.

For about two hours we sat there in furnace temperatures, too exhausted to speak. Then suddenly we all heard it, the glorious sound of an engine. Something was coming. Help was on the way. An enormous two-ton white truck lumbered to a halt as we flagged it down.

"Thank you so much, Lord," I whispered.

Two large Africans in dirt-smeared working clothes slid down from the cab, accompanied by the powerful smell of human sweat. They looked concerned and Patrick explained the situation as they could not speak English. One of them produced a rope and Patrick relayed the good news that they were going to tow us to the police camp at Mushumbi Pools, more than one hundred kilometers (sixty miles) down the road. How we praised God for these two men. Bush people are very aware of the hazards of being stranded and are invariably willing to help strangers in a crisis. So we were hooked up behind their vehicle and embarked on another nightmare journey.

"Please drive slowly," Jerry yelled, but his words were drowned as the truck's powerful engine roared into action and we were catapulted forward. Dust thrown up by the other vehicle engulfed us as we swayed perilously from side to side, coughing and spluttering vigorously. It took immense concentration on Jerry's part to peer through the murk, and every ounce of strength to keep the Land Rover vertical. I closed my eyes, praying fervently that we would arrive at the camp intact.

We arrived at the police camp without mishap and were granted permission to pitch our tent there. After a meal of fried chicken and salad which we had brought from home, Mae and I sat outside our tent watching the light begin to fade. I tried not to think of the next battalion of hazards that could well be assembling in the approaching darkness. It was one thing to cope with wildlife when you could see them, but I did not relish entertaining unseen guests in the night watches.

Mae obviously had anxieties preying on her mind too, for she tentatively began to express her reservations. "Gail, do you ... , er ... , do you think we are safe here? Will we be alright?" she asked falteringly, shifting her slender body restlessly.

Trying to assume the role of great woman of faith, I confidently asserted: "Mae, the Lord is with us, and I am sure everything is going to be fine."

How jealously we guard our reputations and how slow we are to make ourselves vulnerable! It might have been more honest to say: "I know we should be trusting God, but I am absolutely petrified." That would hardly have been much help to Mae, and no purpose would have been served by working each other up into hysteria.

We retired to bed, trusting that there would not be too many challenges facing us in the next few hours, so that we could get some rest. We would need it tomorrow.

We were awakened by a loud shout.

"What was that?" I was instantly awake and sitting upright on my cot.

"Sounds like a gunshot," Jerry replied from his cot next to mine.

"What on earth can be going on?" The other two occupants of our rather cramped four-man tent sounded concerned. We waited with racing hearts. Tales of terrorist killings and other atrocities committed out in remote bush areas filled my mind. Another shot rang out, followed by the voice of one of the policemen at the camp.

"Not to worry! Not to worry! I have just shot a leopard. He is heading your way."

His invitation not to worry hardly seemed appropriate linked to the information that a wounded big cat was probably limping in our direction even now, presumably in a fairly black mood, having found himself the startled recipient of an incredibly fast-moving lump of lead, which was now lodged in his body and was doubtless hurting him like crazy. He could hardly be expected to dole out grace and favor to any members of the human race he happened to bump into that night as he staggered back to his lair for some serious wound-licking.

In Search of the Ostrich People

Wondering whether death at the hands of a terrorist was preferable to being savaged by a leopard with a bullet wound, I sank back on my cot. We suddenly seemed very vulnerable in our tiny tent, but there wasn't much we could do but stare into the pitch blackness and pray. "Oh God," I whispered rather pathetically, "please don't let the leopard get us."

A crunching of leaves convinced me our furry adversary was stealthily creeping towards us. I strained my ears and thought I could hear the sounds of claws scrabbling to get a grip on the bark of the tree under which our tent was pitched. Maybe the policeman had missed, if the leopard was able to cope with climbing trees. I became convinced that we could expect an attack from above any moment.

I wondered what Mae, in the cot next to mine, and her husband were thinking. Maybe they did not have such fertile imaginations. Even though you know that God is taking care of you, sometimes the flesh makes it extremely difficult to accept it fully. Finally I must have drifted off to sleep.

Suddenly I was wide awake again, screaming in terror. Something had touched my arm. I jumped up to escape from the leopard, and the cot promptly collapsed beneath me, leaving my legs waving about in the air. Jerry and the others were helpless with laughter. Apparently Mae had rolled over in her sleep and hit me with her arm, our cots being in such close proximity. I was far from amused. I was unable to move and feared that I might only have escaped the leopard to fall victim to a snake which, for all I knew, could be lurking under the cot right now.

"Jerry, stop laughing and help me," I bleated in a very peeved voice.

We were all relieved when, at last, day dawned and we found that we were unharmed.

We were to spend two more days in Mushumbi Pools. Doug and Patrick caught an African bus into Guruve on Monday to try and locate another battery. We used the time to walk to nearby villages to preach and to talk to the policemen about a living relationship with Jesus Christ. This could have been a time of great frustration and anxiety, but God was at work in an incredible way in that camp, and several policemen became Christians as a result. They even asked us to set up a church in the area, but we had another task to accomplish right then. We were impatient to be on the road again narrowing the distance between us and the mysterious two-toed people.

CHAPTER TWENTY-THREE

A SHY PEOPLE

E ven after the new battery was in place, the Land Rover didn't want to start. "I think it must be the spark plugs," Doug announced. "The acid has corroded them."

Refusing to be discouraged, we bolstered our faith by singing victory songs at full volume, as we packed up the rest of the gear. Sure enough, two hours later we waved good-bye to the policemen and continued our journey.

An hour or so later we were back searching for a jack. Not long after we had left camp, the left rear tire had gone flat, and while Doug was trying to fix it, the jack broke. We could improvise for now, using some rocks and a pole made from a small tree, to lift the Land Rover, but Doug considered it to be very dangerous to continue our journey without a proper jack.

Mushumbi Pools was no more able to provide a spare jack than a battery, and Doug suggested that maybe the time had come to abandon our expedition. To proceed into such a dangerous area with no jack and an ailing vehicle seemed to him sheer folly.

At this stage, however, we were convinced that so much had gone wrong that the only possible explanation was an all-out attempt by the forces of evil to force us to jettison our plans. We were determined not to give in. This was clearly a spiritual battle, and we were going to fight it in Jesus' name.

"We're going on," Jerry declared quietly.

The lug nuts on the wheel were tightened once more, and we headed out for Kanyemba.

After another full day of driving on extremely rough roads, through ever-thickening bush, in blistering temperatures around the one hundred degree mark, we finally made it to the police outpost at Kanyemba. Weary and dirt-stained, all I wanted to do was collapse in a heap. I certainly did not want to face another dilemma.

"What are you doing here?" a policeman asked, seemingly in bewilderment rather than hostility. We were not exactly on the regular tourist trail, and white faces were an unusual sight in that remote area.

"We are looking for the Vadoma people," we answered. "Are they in this area?"

"Yes, they're here, but you will never find them."

We looked at each other with excitement sparkling in our eyes. This was our first indication that we were on the right track and that God had indeed shown us where to find the Vadoma.

"Even the government could not find them when they wanted to enlist them in the army during the war," confirmed another policeman. "They just run off into the hills and hide."

Nothing, not even the improbability of finding these people, could detract from our joy at knowing that we were so near. If God had taken the trouble to reveal their whereabouts in such a wonderful way, we had faith that He would complete the job and enable us to actually find them.

A Shy People

When the policemen knew that we planned to sleep in our own tent in the area, they were incredulous.

"You're not serious?" one policeman said, throwing back his head and roaring with laughter. "You can't pitch a tent there. Lion, leopard and elephant come down every night to drink," he warned, waving his hand towards the nearby glistening waters of the great Zambezi river.

This river, the fourth longest in Africa, and one of the least explored and inhabited in the world, is about one thousand, six hundred miles long from source to mouth and passes through some of the most beautiful scenery in southern Africa. Across the river lay the country of Zambia and, to the northeast, the land of Mozambique.

So we had a major accommodation problem on our hands. There was no hotel around the corner, and the tent was obviously an invitation to the local big game to sample a tempting white-flesh takeout. Not relishing the thought of becoming a convenience food, we turned to God once more for a solution. We did not have long to wait.

"We have got an empty house here if you want to use it," one of the policemen offered. We seized upon this offer without hesitation and proceeded to set up our camp in the simple two-room house. There was not a stick of furniture in the place, but to us it was a palace — until it started to rain, that is.

We awoke in the morning to find our cots floating on a miniature lake. Our clothes and shoes were wet, and as I looked over the side of my cot I realized that we would need some bright sunshine to dry out all our possessions before we could think of moving forward.

We were advised to get permission from Chief Chapoto of the Chikunda tribe to move through his area before continuing our search for the Ostrich People. We passed the telltale brown stains of dried blood on the ground indicating where an animal had recently been killed, and eventually reached a group of women sitting on a bamboo mat under a tree. As we approached, they stopped talking and eyed us suspiciously. Their faces were full of fear. We were possibly the first white people they had ever seen as village women seldom travel far.

Having ascertained that the group included the chief's three wives, we managed to communicate that we would like to see him. Their bodies, enveloped in long lengths of cloth, stiffened. Eventually we realized that the chief was very ill and possibly about to die. Jerry told them that he would like to pray for the chief and, probably deciding that there was not much to lose, one of the women got up and led Doug, Patrick and Jerry to a house constructed of handmade bricks.

A pale, mud-colored dog with protruding ribs bared its teeth, barked halfheartedly and then slunk off behind one of the neatly thatched huts clustered together on the light brown sand. Chickens scratched idly at the ground, pessimistic about finding anything to eat, and scrawny goats wandered listlessly around the village well.

The grass-roofed huts nearby constituted the bedrooms of the chief's wives, a kitchen and a small room for grinding corn. The only other brick structure in the village was a roughly constructed schoolhouse with openings for windows.

Resisting the temptation to back out when the stench of the unwashed, sick body hit them, and the smoke from the cooking fire stung their eyes, the men entered the dark room. As their eyes grew accustomed to the darkness, they saw the thin, wrinkled body of the old chief lying on a small bed. He was naked to the waist, and the rest of his body was covered by a dirty cloth. He had obviously been suffering from a high fever, probably caused by malaria, and was now dehydrated and extremely weak. Doug, Jerry and Patrick prayed for him, and immediately God touched him and he was healed and got up to speak with them.

"Why have you come to my village?" he inquired.

"We want to meet with the Vadoma people," Jerry explained.

"What do you want with the Vadoma?" the old man asked warily.

"We want to tell them about Jesus Christ. The same Jesus Christ who has just made you well," Jerry replied.

"You can go, but I doubt whether you'll find them," the chief responded.

At this point the four men emerged from the hut and rejoined us. We praised God to see the chief standing there obviously no longer on the verge of death. He was pointing to an area of tall elephant grass which stood way above our heads, probably indicating that we would find the Vadoma people in that direction. I tried to pull down a shutter on my imagination which had automatically begun to create a lurid picture of all the dangers concealed in that thick grass.

The chief was now quite close. Suddenly I noticed a small man in a very ragged shirt and shorts coming out of the bush towards us. "There is one of the Vadoma coming now," exclaimed the chief and went over to talk to the man.

We watched this dirt-encrusted, sweat-stained man with protruding teeth in fascinated wonder. Here, actually standing in front of us, was a member of this self-conscious people we had come so far to meet, a people whose very existence was denied by those born and bred in Zimbabwe, a people God had spoken to us about through a magazine article in far-off America. The fact that this man had walked out of the bush at this precise moment filled me with an enormous sense of awe. I silently worshipped God for the amazing privilege of being involved in His incredible plans.

The man looked less than enthusiastic about meeting us but, after a considerable amount of rapid dialogue and fevered gesticulation, the chief announced: "I have told him who you are, and he has agreed to lead you back to his village."

Even the chief seemed slightly taken aback at developments. "You must get out of there before dark," he continued. "It is extremely dangerous. The lions and other wild animals will attack you. Make sure you're back before dark." And we went off in a line behind the Vadoma man.

It wasn't long before a new problem emerged. Patrick, after attempting to speak to the Vadoma man, returned to us and said, "Pastor, I don't understand this man. He doesn't speak Tonga, and we can't understand each other. They lied to you about the language the Vadoma speak. What are we going to do now? What is the point of getting all the way to the people and then not being able to preach to them?" He was clearly agitated by this turn of events.

We had been following the Vadoma man for some time, our faces lightly slapped by the eight-feet-tall elephant grass, and our bodies exposed to the direct glare of the sun's blistering rays. "Well," replied Jerry, "All I know how to do is pray. God has achieved so many miracles to get us this far, I'm sure He will come up with something."

After a brief prayer we walked on silently, our clothes uncomfortably wet from the perspiration that poured down our faces and backs. Our legs felt leaden and sometimes it seemed that we didn't have enough energy to keep putting one foot in front of the other. I wondered how our guide kept going. It was all so effortless for him, although he didn't look like he had eaten a square meal for weeks.

Gradually the sheer effort of keeping going absorbed my mind completely, blotting out fears of snakebite or being grabbed by a snack-hunting wild beast. "Lord, You have given us a job to do, and all I want is to be obedient to You," I prayed. "Please help me to keep going."

After nearly three hours of walking through the interminable grass and across crocodile-infested river beds, our hearts leapt. There in the distance were some huts. Our pace quickened with an excitement that caused the physical discomfort to fade for a moment. At last we were in sight of the Vadoma.

Suddenly a loud shout split the air. I realized it was Patrick. Had he spotted a lion? Had he been bitten?

"What on earth is the matter?" I cried.

"Pastor! Pastor!" Patrick yelled. "God has just given me the language. I can understand this man now, and he can understand me. I don't know what has happened, but I know what he is saying."

We were totally dumbfounded. God, in an incredibly gracious way, had intervened so that communication with the Ostrich People would be possible. Once more we were humbled at being involved in such an important part of God's purposes. What great love God had for these people we were about to meet — or were we?

As we entered the village, everything was eerily quiet. The place seemed to sit deserted in the shimmering heat. We did find a few people home, the very elderly and others too sick to move. The Vadoma people, we learned, are not farmers and, since many legal constraints had been placed on hunting, large numbers of them were suffering from malnutrition.

But our presence was viewed by many eyes, we were to later learn. The able-bodied among the Vadoma had hidden in the bushes, too frightened to meet us.

We left a message with those we met, explaining that we would come back on Saturday to tell everyone about a Man who wanted to help them, a Man called Jesus. If they wanted to hear this good news, we asked them to meet us under a certain tree in Chief Chapoto's village that day. We could only pray that many would come.

By now it was getting late, and we had a long trek ahead of us. Our guide accompanied us part of the way and then asked if we could manage without him. There was not enough time for him to complete the round trip journey by nightfall, and he did not want to be stranded. We agreed.

Tired, thirsty and exhausted, we finally limped out of the bush and back to the safety of the police camp. Initial disappointment had been replaced by a sense of jubilation and faith. Everyone had said that it was an impossible task to find the Ostrich People, but our great God had enabled us to make contact with them, and we were confident that what He had started He would complete.

CHAPTER TWENTY-FOUR

MURDER AND ITS VICTIMS

Our time was well spent as we waited for our Saturday appointment. One day, as we stood, viewing the Zambezi, small insects danced a strange ritual in the air like a mobile in a child's room responding to a faint breeze. I scanned the river but could see no sign of a boat. The dark, bulky shapes of several half-submerged hippopotamuses caught my eye, and an unnerving number of log-like crocodiles seemed to be floating with an air of innocence on the surface of the Zambezi. The banks of this mighty river are home to some of Africa's most prolific game herds.

"Where is your boat?" I asked a young man whom we had met at the police camp. As it turned out, he was a backslidden Christian and, after recommitting his life to Christ, he had invited us to cross the river into Zambia to bring the Gospel to his family.

We were certainly not lacking activities, but we decided to accept his invitation. We had brought no passports and we had no visas to enter Zambia, but the police gave us permission to make the brief trip across the river.

"There it is," the young man rejoined, pointing to a hollowed-out tree trunk canoe hauled up on the shore. My heart sank. I could not imagine how this frail craft was going to negotiate the river given the size of our group. I would have doubted its capacity for reaching the other side with seven small children let alone seven normal-sized adults.

As I gingerly put a foot into that dangerously wobbly boat I have to confess I was terrified. Every last vision of bravely going out in the name of the Lord, intrepid to the end, evaporated swiftly. At that moment I would have given anything to be at a kitchen sink in some comfortable house somewhere. I just wanted to be doing safe and ordinary things, not crossing a river in a log canoe. The great woman of God, full of faith and vision, was once again nowhere to be seen.

I grimly clung to the side of the boat, determined not to show my fear.

"Don't do that. Move your hands at once, " I was instructed sharply.

"Why?" I asked meekly, slightly annoyed at being ordered around like a schoolgirl.

"The crocodiles will take your fingers," was the swift reply.

I wasted no time in complying and spent the rest of the trip in fervent prayer for survival.

Maybe courage is not a question of sailing through life with no fears, but choosing to trust God and get on with the task at hand — even when our heart is fluttering wildly.

I was extremely grateful to God that we avoided any close encounter with fast-snapping jaws and were able to bring the message of new life in Jesus Christ to the people we met in Zambia.

On the return river crossing, we heard a shot and later learned that a hippopotamus had tried to overturn a police boat. We waved good-bye to Zambia and landed thankfully on Zimbabwean soil, just as it was getting dark. Soon we were back in the relative security of the police camp.

A very sad thing happened while we were still staying in the camp. One morning, very early, I became dimly aware of a noise, noise that was trying to drag me out of a comfortable place that I did not want to leave. I desperately wanted it to stop. Finally, the high-pitched screaming of a baby forced me into full consciousness.

"Are you awake, Jerry?"

He grunted a noncommittal reply.

"What do you think is going on?" I persisted.

"Don't know," he responded sleepily. "What's the time?" he added after a brief pause.

"About three-thirty," I replied.

Voices were raised, and the baby continued to scream. Exhausted after our trek the previous day into Zambian villages, we lay still, unable to summon the strength to go and investigate what was happening outside. Gradually the commotion died down, people moved away, and the sound of crying grew fainter. After a while, we drifted back to sleep.

Early in the morning a policeman came to the door. "Can you help us, Mother? We have no milk," he pleaded. He was carrying a baby whose face was puckered in a frightful grimace as it howled with hunger. I noticed brown stains on its clothing.

"What on earth has happened?" I asked in some consternation.

"It is a terrible business," he said and seemed reluctant to talk about it further. I noticed a little girl, with fear in her eyes, standing silently nearby. We finally established that a man had brutally attacked and killed his wife with an axe, leaving terrible wounds in her back, neck and the side of her face. The baby had been clinging to her back when this tragic incident occurred. The only other witness was the little six-year-old girl whose name, the policeman told me, was Shupikayi which means "suffering." *What a horribly appropriate name under the circumstances!* I thought, for I could scarcely conceive of greater suffering than this child had already experienced at such an impressionable age.

I later learned that the child had run to the well for water, pouring it over her mother's body in a futile effort to revive her, crying out all the while, "Amai! Amai!" (Mother! Mother!) The dead woman's body was now lying in the empty house next door.

Holding the three-month-old baby in my arms, I took the children indoors, having promised the policeman I would do all I could to help them.

I found tears pricking my eyes, and there was a terrible ache in my heart as I looked at these poor traumatized children. I had no idea what to do. I had no baby bottle, no milk and no diapers. There was nothing in this wilderness with which to care for a small baby. "Help me, Lord," I cried.

Then I remembered I had some Cremora powdered milk. We had brought it with us to add to our coffee. I mixed some of the Cremora with water and fed the baby with a spoon. Soon, he stopped crying. I cut up some of our towels to make diapers for him.

I held Shupikayi in my arms and sang softly to her: "Jesus loves me. This I know, for the Bible tells me so." As I sang I tried to comprehend what it must be like to be suddenly and violently separated from your mother, to try and revive her bleeding body, desperate to make her speak again and then to find yourself with strange people with white faces who cannot understand what you are saying. All this when you are only six years old. It was too much. I cried out to God with a breaking heart for these two bereaved children.

A nurse was brought from a clinic, thirty minutes' drive away. She watched over the dead woman's body until it was removed to Guruve. She also helped with the children who would be taken to Guruve too so that their future could be decided.

CHAPTER TWENTY-FIVE

THE DAY ARRIVES

On Saturday morning, I awoke very excited. This was the day we had been waiting for so long. Today we would meet the Vadoma people. Hippos bellowed somewhere in the distance as I got up, washed and dressed for the day.

Dozens of questions coursed through my mind: Would the people turn up? Was it reasonable to expect them to come so far after such a casual initial contact? How would they respond if they did come? We had been repeatedly told about their secretive ways and how they shied away from involvement with all groups of people.

Once again, I reviewed in my mind all that God had done to bring us to this point. It was considerable, and even if the people did not come today, we would not give up. We would go back into the bush if necessary to tell them about Jesus.

The thirty-minute drive to the chief's village seemed to take an inordinately long time. As we got nearer, my mouth was dry and my heart felt as if it was going to explode. At last we approached the final hill. In a moment we would know the answer to some of our questions.

We reached the brow of the incline and the tree we

had designated as a meeting area came into view. Hardly able to believe our eyes, our hearts swelled with praise, for under the shade of that tree we could see many, many people waiting for us. "Oh God," I rejoiced, "You've done it! You've brought the people!"

There were about one hundred and twenty Vadoma and thirty Chikunda people gathered to hear for the first time in their lives the story of how God sent His Son Jesus Christ to express His deep love for us. The first thing we did was teach them a song "Ndinotenda Jesu" (Thank You Jesus). Then Jerry preached a very simple message. When he finished, he asked those who wanted to accept Jesus to come forward, but no one moved.

Because of the great silence under the mighty branches of the tree, Jerry told me later that he had cried out to God in utter despair: "Oh God, I've missed it. After all the miracles You have performed to get us here, I somehow have failed to make the message clear. What do I do now?" And God began to drop a solution into Jerry's mind.

He picked up a stick and knelt on the ground. Drawing pictures in the sand, he began to tell the story of Jesus again. The Africans love stories, and they eagerly leaned forward, listening attentively to every word. Finally the chief spoke: "Why do we need this man? We have our own gods."

Jerry explained once again and asked a second time if anyone wanted to come forward. By the end of that day one hundred and twenty Vadoma people had indicated that they wanted to follow Jesus. No words can adequately express the deep joy we all felt.

The people were keen to learn more about the greatest of all spirits, Jehovah, and they promised to make a road back into their village so that the people too shy to come that day could hear the Gospel too. We distributed food items and clothing to them and finally left for our temporary home at the police camp, talking excitedly about all God had done as we bounced along.

Later that evening as I stood quietly looking out over the Zambezi, I can remember how my spirit soared in praise to God. "Lord, You have done such mighty things. This morning, a whole tribe of people had no idea about You and now, tonight, one hundred and twenty of them have been born into Your Kingdom because of Your incredible faithfulness."

I thought about the people in Zambia who had responded to the message and all those along the way who wanted to know about Jesus. In my mind I travelled back to the church in America where God had touched my heart. I heard the voice of that evangelist: "What are you asking God for? Are you asking for a new home? Are you asking for success in real estate? Are you asking for a Lincoln Continental? It is all trash. 'Ask for the heathen for thine inheritance,' says God, 'and I will give you the uttermost parts of the Earth.' "

"Thank You! Thank You, Lord," I whispered. "You promised that if I would give everything to You, then You would give me far more than I could imagine, and You have. Thank You!"

That night, with a face streaked with dirt and a tired sweaty body being attacked by myriads of biting bugs, I felt like a millionaire. I would not have exchanged places with anyone in the whole world. The sight of those primitive people responding to the love of God was the most glorious experience anyone could ever wish for. I knew that I would never forget that day and that nothing would ever compare with the quality of joy we discovered in being used of God in that place.

Yes, it had been tough, and fear and discomfort might have caused us to turn back, but God, our Father, had enabled us to trust Him to see us through. This was only the beginning of the Church among the Vadoma people.

Chapter Twenty-Six

Exile and Return

We were brought back to reality by the arrival of a policeman who had returned from Guruve with the children. It seemed that no one there was in a position to look after them.

"What will happen to them then?" I asked.

"Well, I expect the baby will die," he replied, "but the little girl might survive as she is older."

My heart felt as if it would break. We could not leave these children here to die. "Would you let me take them?" I asked.

"Well, I suppose if you want them, there is nothing to stop you," the policeman replied, looking relieved at a possible solution to his problem.

I was thinking of a Christian children's home at Concession, north of Harare, called Montgomery Heights. I had helped them to set up a Christian school there and had visited it on a number of occasions. I knew they didn't take babies, but someone had to care for these children. We cried to God that He would overcome the difficulties and provide a home for these traumatized little ones.

We took a break in our packing to watch a breathtaking sunrise over Mozambique. Then it was time to head for home.

Exile and Return

Before we could leave, a police official told us that they had decided to keep Shupikayi, who we later renamed Joy, because she would be needed in the future for questioning. Afraid that we would never see her again and concerned for her ultimate safety, we persuaded the police that it was better to keep the children together after all they had been through. We pointed out that they could always visit her in Concession if they needed to ask further questions. In the end they agreed to let us take her. So we commenced our journey back over the same rough, gruelling roads, amazed at how resilient the children were to the discomforts.

After what seemed like an eternity, we at last turned into Montgomery Heights and poured out our story with some trepidation to Martin and Margaret Emerson who ran the children's home. Margaret didn't seem altogether surprised to see us and when we had finished we discovered why.

"One of the African staff came to me about three days ago," she explained. "This lady told me that God had showed her that He was going to send us a small baby."

We were thrilled that God had prepared the people at Montgomery for the arrival of these children and realized that it had been exactly three days before when we started caring for them. Driving back to Harare we felt secure in the knowledge that the children were safe in the hands of God's people.

Today, Benjamin, the baby, is fourteen years old and Joy is twenty-one. She is my best interpreter when I teach or preach. Both of these young people know the Lord and serve Him. Not only were their physical lives spared when God took us to Kanyemba, but they also received new life spiritually as a result.

We returned to Kanyemba many times in the coming years and saw God work in ways that amazed us. Today there are about twenty-five churches in the area. The student, Patrick, who accompanied us on that first eventful trip, later became a pastor of those people and remained there faithfully serving God for many years. We managed to get Bible translators to work there, and now part of the New Testament is available in the Chikunda language.

Water baptism was an unusual challenge for the Vadoma who were understandably frightened of the crocodile-infested rivers, which also hosted snakes and a whole range of disease-causing parasites. In the thinking of the Vadoma, water was associated with disease and death. Still these people had a deep desire to obey the teachings of the Christian faith.

The baptism itself was quite interesting. An area of the river was cordoned off by a chain of dugouts moored end to end, and a team of beaters with reeds vigorously thrashed the murky waters to warn off marauding crocodiles. The tribal headman, Chiambo, relaxed in the arms of the pastor who was going to baptize him and asked: "Are you really going to drown me?"

With a shock, the pastor realized that these people actually thought that baptism involved death by drowning, but that if they were obedient, Jesus Christ Himself would bring them back to life through His mighty power. Their desire to be baptized took on a whole new significance as we realized the depth of their faith in God and the innocent trust they had placed in us.

As the months passed, miracle after miracle happened at Kanyemba, bringing many people to faith in Christ. A small girl who had died was restored to life. She had been sick for a long time, and one day, when Patrick was teaching the Vadoma to make bricks, news came that she had finally died. Patrick was taken to the dead child and, kneeling down, he prayed, and life returned to the small body stretched out before him. Such were the miracles that God did in that place!

The home of the Vadoma people was also the seat of ancestral worship, and it was not long before the witch doctors became seriously concerned about the inroads God's Kingdom was making on their territory. The result was a violent confrontation between the powers of evil and the Holy Spirit which reached a climax when, unknown to us, new officials took government office in the area.

Suddenly, we found ourselves banned from the area, accused of being spies and engaging in subversive political activities. Warned that if we attempted to enter the region by air we would be shot down and that we would be apprehended at checkpoints if we attempted a land route, we were also asked to evacuate the pastor. Patrick, however, refused to leave his people declaring fearlessly: "If it costs me my life, I am not coming out. God has put me here and no man is going to remove me."

The Vadoma people wanted us to stay, but authorities lied to them, telling them that their missionaries had abandoned and betrayed them. Patrick continually reassured the people that our commitment had not faltered, and that we were being prevented by the government from making regular visits.

During the time of our exile we continually cried to God that He would defeat our enemies and open the way into Kanyemba again. Eventually, after two years,

He answered our prayers. The government officials who opposed us lost their jobs and those who had supported what we were doing in the area were reinstated. Once again we had access to the place where we had witnessed so many miracles of God.

We learned so much through the experience of bringing the Gospel to the Vadoma people, and not all of what we learned was positive. It wasn't long before people began to try to capitalize on the noteriety of the two-toed people.

As news of what God was doing filtered out to the wider Christian community, we began to be bombarded with offers of help and requests to visit the area. Since we urgently needed finances to complete the projects we had started to improve the quality of life for these people, we accepted all comers, being naive enough to believe that all offers of help were genuine. We took many people into the area and large, well-known ministries made extravagant promises of help, but much of that promised help never materialized.

One organization ran a feature article about the Ostrich People in their magazine, and raised thousands of dollars for our work. When only a fraction of what was given reached us, we took the matter up with the organization and were informed that it was their policy to give a one-time donation, regardless of how much came in for a specific project.

Plenty of people were anxious to identify with us in this project when the going was easy, but they suddenly melted away, taking their money with them, when the threats of death and government hostility began. When the ban was finally lifted, we were back in fashion and the calls requesting visits and offers of help were resumed, as if nothing had happened in the meantime.

Gradually, we learned to be more selective about those we allowed to be involved in the work. These incidents, although casting a shadow over the situation, could never detract significantly from the wonder of being involved in this miracle.

We have never ceased to praise God for allowing us the privilege of being there when He revealed Himself to a tribe of people who had never heard the name of Jesus, and we praise Him, as well, that down through the years the work in that area of Zimbabwe has continued to be powerful and lasting — despite intense opposition.

CHAPTER TWENTY-SEVEN

ENLARGE YOUR BORDERS

W hen God spoke to us to begin a massive new building project at Living Waters Bible College, I was very reluctant. Jerry is a visionary and accepts the impossible, while my administrative mind wants to reason everything out. Therefore when God said to buy a twenty-five acre horse farm and turn it into a Bible college, the $180,000 asking price was no problem for Jerry — although we had only $200 at the time. It took me a little longer to accept.

One day God said to me, "Gail, offer them $165,000 cash." (My background in real estate has come in handy more than once in the ministry.) A tremendous battle ensued in my heart before I obeyed. This represented a big step of faith. I needed to know that this was the voice of God and not simply a good idea. Then I could stand the storms of doubt which later might surface as the burden of administration would fall on me while Jerry made a visit to America to share the vision.

Through many miracles we were able to pay well over $100,000 during the next three months, but when the pressure to pay the balance became heavy, although I knew that God was doing the work, I still felt sick each time the phone rang and I reached for the receiver. How could I explain faith to the lawyer representing the sellers? How should I say we were planning to pay the balance?

"Mrs. Rozell, when will the money be available? This is becoming a matter of great urgency," I heard him say, but I had nothing concrete to tell him and when his calls became a daily occurrence, I grew discouraged.

I decided to talk over my predicament with a local pastor whose church we attended when we were not out in ministry of our own. He was famous for his faith teaching. *Surely he could encourage me and give me some direction,* I thought. I was to be sorely disappointed.

After hearing my story, the man, instead of sharing with me some encouraging words, wondered out loud if we had not acted presumptuously in this matter, rather than hearing the voice of God. I left his office that day rather shaken.

God, however, was right on time. Seven months from the time we started the project, the new sight was dedicated to the Lord, totally debt free. Jerry could not help gloating a little with our faith friend later. The man was now excited about what had been done. "I knew it was God from the beginning," Jerry told him, smiling.

Later we remodeled the horse stables, making dormitories, and built classrooms, a library, offices and a chapel, before turning the college over to the national leaders debt free. The total cost had been more than a million dollars, and God had provided faithfully.

Faith in God is such a powerful force! It had taken us to India and Pakistan; it had brought us through many difficult situations at home and abroad; it had enabled us to bring the Gospel to the Vadoma people; it had enabled us to build the new Bible college; and it would be the key to the next move in our lives.

CHAPTER TWENTY-EIGHT

MOTHER OF MANY NATIONS

I got a glimpse of what was coming one day when a young Chinese teacher who had been staying with us suddenly asked me, "May I call you Mother?"

I looked up in surprise. We had been about to start lunch when he had suddenly, for no apparent reason, asked this question.

Brushing back a straying lock of thick black hair, he continued, "My family is Buddhist, and I have often wondered what it would be like to have a Christian mother. I have lived with you for some time and watched the way you live. I see that you are everything I thought a Christian mother would be. Do you mind if I call you Mother?"

I watched a mud wasp amble across the window ledge and felt humbled by the words this slight young man sitting opposite me had spoken. Only too well aware of my shortcomings, I found it hard to respond as a lump seemed to rise in my throat. Once again I remembered God's promise to me as a young girl — that I would be the mother of many nations. Although I had battled with my inability to bear children of my own, God had other ways of accomplishing His purposes. The words of this young man and the memories of God's faithfulness moved me greatly.

Realizing that my long silence might be misunderstood, I looked over and smiled at my new son. "Of course you can call me Mother," I replied.

When I made that statement, I had no idea, as yet, the length to which God would extend my family, and that was probably a good thing. It wasn't long before I became deeply involved in a much larger project, a project to save the Montgomery Heights children's home.

Sometime before we had taken Joy and Benjamin to live in that home, Martin and Margaret Emerson had told us that they were planning to go abroad and felt it was time to relinquish their positions at the home. So far, they had not been successful in their search for someone to fill their shoes. One day Martin informed us, "I have tried everything, but no one is prepared to take on the work. If Montgomery Heights has to close I don't know what will become of the children."

I had begun to make regular visits there, and eventually became part of the management team for the home. Through my visits I had come to know many of the children personally. Although their numbers had diminished in recent months, I could not bear the thought of the remaining children being turned out of the home. Most of them, like Joy and Benjamin, had already experienced too much pain, insecurity and rejection in their lives.

Jerry and I had the responsibility of the Bible college and the oversight of various local churches, so taking on a children's home in addition to our other work seemed out of the question. My heart sank, however, at the thought of the home having to close. One day, as I was leaving the home, I said, rather vaguely and tentatively, to Martin, "Martin, get back to me if you still cannot find anyone to take on Montgomery."

When time passed and no help was found, Jerry and I had to take a deep breath and throw ourselves on the mercy of the God of impossibilities. We were now responsible for the Montgomery Heights children's home and all that responsibility entailed.

In stages, we left Living Waters Bible College in other capable hands and moved fifty miles to the north to rural Zimbabwe and the thirty-five acre site of the home. Over time, many new children came to the home to receive love and care. And many people helped us to provide that care, giving their time, their talents and their money. Many of the farmers who live in that predominantly agricultural area have given generously to the support of the home. So that we not only saved the work, but have been able to expand it.

Most of the children who have come to us have been damaged by physical, mental or sexual abuse. Some of them have been orphaned by the death of parents who had AIDS. Some of them were abandoned and left along remote roadsides with nothing to eat or drink. Some were terribly malnourished, not having eaten for days. Many have come to us with nothing but the tattered rags they were wearing. Each one of these children is loved by God and it has been a privilege to be Mom and Dad to them.

Our Christian school, operating on the Accelerated Christian Education program, is flourishing. There is a clinic on site which treats people in the local community and many churches and Bible study groups are under our care in the surrounding area.

Montgomery Heights has been, for us, a place of much joy and laughter, but it has also been a place of tears. Take, for instance, the case of Norbert.

CHAPTER TWENTY-NINE

NORBERT'S STORY

The powerful African sun was blazing down from a blue sky the day that three-year-old Norbert arrived at Montgomery Heights. He marched boldly up to me with a big smile on his face and shook my hand rather quaintly. He showed great promise. But this friendly little boy, with eyes that sparkled with the sheer joy of living, would prove to be a source of unbearable suffering for all of us in the days to come.

He had been found with matted hair and filthy clothes in a small village. A tumor had grown behind his eye and a health care worker had taken him to Howard Hospital, our nearest mission hospital run by the Salvation Army. The tumor was removed and Norbert was given chemotherapy and radiation treatments. The hospital environment was hardly the best aid to a small boy's recovery and the matron asked us if we would be prepared to take him.

We thought long and hard before taking on this responsibility. Norbert would have to be taken the fifty miles to Harare once a month for treatment. This would involve leaving him there for three days and making the return journey to bring him back. Back at Montgomery we would have to cope with his sickness and disorientation. It was a large commitment of time when there were many other children to be cared for. "Lord, show us what to do for Norbert," we prayed.

Our hearts were melted by the mere thought of such a small child facing cancer alone, helpless and afraid. We knew that caring for him would be tough, but at least he would be loved and would know that Jesus loved him, too.

At one point, our sacrifice on Norbert's behalf seemed to be greatly rewarded. Doctors proclaimed him free of cancer and his treatment was discontinued. One day I rejoiced as I saw him singing in the classroom with the other children.

It was peaceful as I walked under the date palm tree where the weaver birds' nests, created with such skill by these feathered craftsmen, hung like giant fruits. Sounds of lively singing floated out from the school classroom. Moving closer I watched, unobserved, as Norbert, placing his little hands on his hips, wiggled down to the ground and up again. "I love You, Jesus, deep down in my heart," the children sang. This was his favorite song and getting the actions right was serious business. How wonderful it was to see him enjoying life again!

Later that day he bounded up to me, squeezed me tight and embarked on a long conversation about what he had been doing . Norbert was making his way deeper and deeper into our hearts.

One day I noticed that he seemed rather subdued.

"How's my boy?" I asked.

Instead of his usual cheerful, "I'm fine," he said: "Go-Go (grandmother), my eye is sore."

Fear clutched at my heart. "Let me look, Norbie."

A small piece of white skin seemed to be growing in

the corner of his eye. We had him examined, and the doctor told us that there was nothing wrong, but within a short time the eye began to swell, and he experienced great pain. We decided we had better put him in the Land Cruiser and take him to the hospital.

He loved to ride in the Land Cruiser, but when we had to leave him in the hospital, he cried pitifully and clung to us. Tearing ourselves away from that tear-stained little boy was a terrible thing and felt so cruel, but we had many others to care for. We could only cry to God to comfort him and spare his life. In the coming months, we had to leave him many times, and each occasion seemed, if possible, more heart-rending than the last.

Eventually doctors decided to remove Norbert's eye. It was a traumatic experience, but he seemed to bounce back from it extremely well. Our hopes rose as he came home again and was soon laughing, playing and singing, "I love You, Jesus, deep down in my heart."

Our interlude of happiness was all too short-lived, as Norbert's tumor began to grow again, this time outside the eye socket. Having prayed and prayed for his healing, we took him back to the hospital. And, crying our own desperate tears, we drove home once again without him. He was so small and vulnerable. It was agony to leave him there. All we could see was a little boy crying and begging us to take him home. "Oh God," we prayed, "this is terrible. Please help Norbie. Please heal him."

All the staff at Montgomery pleaded with God for Norbert's life with as much love and fervor as if he had been their own child. Yet the situation got worse.

Surgeons operated on Norbie again, removing the

tumor, but it soon returned, causing him intense pain and discomfort. Watching this little darling suffer tore at our hearts and became an ache beyond words to describe. Sometimes I would hold him gently in my arms for hours, praying for him, singing to him, and reading his favorite books and Bible stories. This made it all the more difficult to leave him when the time came.

The staff at the hospital were always very busy and were not able to give Norbert the attention he needed. On one particular occasion, I had lost my temper over it.

Norbert had been thirsty and there was no cup to give him a drink. I noticed a carton of fruit juice I had brought for him a few days earlier standing unopened on the locker by his bed. "Nurse, could I have a cup to give Norbert a drink?" I inquired.

"Sorry, I'm busy," was the frosty reply, and she swept on down the corridor.

I was seething with anger, and when she returned I was there ready to accost her. "I will get the drink. All I want you to do is show me where I can find a cup."

"I haven't time," she responded in an offhand manner, and with that, something snapped in me.

"To you, this child may only be a small black orphan whom nobody wants. You may not think he deserves your time. To me, he happens to be a very important person. If you don't show me where to get a cup so that this suffering child can have a drink, then I'm telling you that you will regret it."

Looking rather shocked at this outburst and realizing I was probably a force to be reckoned with, she produced a cup in record time and without a word disappeared again.

Norbert's Story

As I retreated with my trophy, I felt sad that I had become so angry. "Father, I'm sorry, but I can't bear the way they are treating him."

Later I had the chance to apologize for how I had spoken, and she too apologized, recognizing my love and anxiety for Norbert.

Norbert bore his pain with amazing courage for so small a boy. His unselfish concern for others was very moving. One day two of our coworkers at Montgomery, Jean Webster and Lesley Marshall, accompanied me when I went to visit him. Although Jean lives at Montgomery, she travels throughout the rural areas of Zimbabwe setting up Christian community orphan support projects. She had recently broken her arm and Norbert, noting the plaster cast, wanted to know what had happened. When Jean had finished relating her story, his face filled with pity and, reaching out his hand, he touched the cast. "Miss Webster, I will pray for you," he said. "Lord Jesus, please will You take away Miss Webster's pain. Amen."

Tears rolled down my cheeks. Here was a six-year-old in great pain himself and yet unselfish enough to pray for someone else. What an example! I noticed that Jean and Lesley were quietly wiping their eyes too.

One day I said to the doctor, "Please be straight with me. If there is anything else you can do for Norbert then please do it, whatever the cost. If not, then please tell me so that I can take him home."

The doctor studied the desk, unable to meet my eyes. "I'm afraid we have lost this one," he told me softly.

Brokenhearted, we took Norbert home to Montgomery, determined to love and care for him to the end. Pete Norris, a qualified nurse, and his wife Sarah took most of the responsibility for nursing the child. This young couple from Britain, who had two children of their own, had been working with us for a couple of years. They cared for Norbert with all the tenderness and compassion of Jesus. The grotesque growth had disfigured his beautiful face beyond description, but day by day they cleaned and cared for him, weeping as they did so.

We watched him grow weaker as his dose of morphine increased until he could no longer move or eat. Yet he would still smile and sometimes even try to sing. We had never given up hope for Norbert and still prayed for a miracle, but God showed us very clearly one Sunday morning that it was time to release Norbert back to Him.

Norbert did not usually complain, but on that Sunday afternoon when I asked him, "How's my boy?" He whispered, "Go-Go, I'm poorly."

At 5:00 a.m. the next morning, Marie, a volunteer helper from the States who was with us for six months, checked and found that Norbert was sleeping. But at 6:00 a.m., when Pete went into the child's room, Norbert had already slipped away to Jesus.

The hours that followed were so difficult. Pete broke the news to me and took me to see him. The doctor who was called to issue the death certificate was not a Christian, but he wept as he did his job, saying, "I just don't know how you do this."

Pete washed Norbert for the last time and laid his body in a little wooden casket, and later that same day it was time to lay Norbert's body in the ground.

Two powder blue waxbills flew up into the trees. I watched the children file solemnly out of their houses and across the grass to the chapel. "Lord, please help them to cope with this," I prayed. "Take away their fears."

They took their places on the rough cain chairs as social workers, local farmers and our staff joined us. Soon the room was packed with people. This brave soldier had touched many lives in his short six years of life.

Hendry, one of the children, leaned over to speak to me. "What is in the box?"

"It is Norbert's body, Hendry, but he is not there. He is with Jesus."

Norbert's relatives sat huddled together looking uncomfortable. They had not seen the child in three years, and yet had wanted us to perform all the traditional African rites such as turning the coffin around. They believed this would prevent the spirits from finding him. We insisted on a Christian funeral.

The children gathered around the casket and sang, led by Joy, "I love You, Jesus, deep down in my heart."

Later, four of the older boys carried the rose-covered casket out into the sunshine, and we laid him to rest in the rich red earth of Montgomery Heights.

There is so much that I do not understand about his passing, but I feel so privileged to have known Norbert and to know that he loved me. I am so glad that we were able to teach him to love Jesus, and that now he is safe in the arms of his Saviour. I know that one day I will see him again. He will probably be wiggling his hips and singing, "I love You, Jesus." Who knows?

Sometimes I have wished that I was a lot tougher and that these children did not wrench at my heart so painfully.

CHAPTER THIRTY

OUR MIRACLE BOY AND OTHERS

When Joseph was handed to me by the nurse, he was a miserable-looking baby. Wet, dirty and bald, he was dressed in some adult-sized hospital issue pajamas, and his face was puckered in a pre-howl grimace.

Obviously he didn't find me very attractive either because, taking one look at my face, he began to scream uncontrollably and tried to escape from my arms. I was probably the first white person he had ever encountered, and he seemed determined to make sure I was the last.

I called Mrs. Muleya, the African housemother of the toddler's home, as I thought this might calm the situation. And it worked. Sliding into her arms, he stopped crying, pacified by the familiar sight of black skin.

A telephone call had come several days earlier from the social welfare agency asking if we would take a baby whose mother had died. I agreed. No one told me at the time that the child had tested HIV positive.

It hurt me to see Joseph's fear of me, so I set out to change things. Each day I held him and walked round the garden singing to him and praying for him. I told this nine-month-old baby that he was special and I loved him. I told him that Jesus loved him, too. Gradually a bond developed between us that I believe will last forever.

As Joseph grew, he would try to sing with me. At first he could only garble out words which I finally recognized as "Bible" and "Jesus," but one day he managed a whole song. But he wasn't growing as he should, and he was often sick. Constant diarrhoea kept him weak, although we gave him vitamins and special foods to nourish him. He had to be prayed back from the brink of death so many times that we came to call him our miracle boy.

When he was three, Joseph became more seriously ill. For two weeks he was racked with pain and high fever. He had severe diarrhoea and was so weakened that he could not walk. Pete came to me and said gently: "Gail, I know that you don't want to hear this, but there is nothing more I can do for Joseph."

I knew that he was right. It was amazing that we had kept the child so long, but my heart was broken, despite my efforts to accept the facts and subdue my emotions.

On Sunday, I sat in the service with Joe on my lap. My dress was wet from the perspiration that poured from his little fevered body. Whenever I moved, he cried. The chapel was filled with the rich melody of Lesley's voice singing "Only Jesus has the power." The truth of those words moved me, and I began to weep before God. I prayed, "Oh Jesus, only You have the power to touch Joseph. Will You please touch him once more? I know the facts, but, please, Jesus, touch his body."

Jerry called the elders, and they anointed Joseph with oil and prayed. To my amazement, the fever immediately began to abate, and I watched his condition improve during the rest of the day.

The next day an ugly boil appeared in Joseph's groin.

Pete drained it and the infection disappeared. Before long the child was running and skipping around Montgomery with the other toddlers.

Then, about eighteen months later, Joseph again became extremely ill. This time the doctor decided that a second killer disease was at work in his body, Sickle Cell Anaemia. Joseph had to be placed in our high care unit for twenty-four hour nursing. This was extremely difficult for us, since it had not been long since Norbert had died there.

As I had with Norbert, I sat for hours holding this child and praying. When I tried to leave him, he would cling to me and cry, bringing back all the memories of the painful partings from Norbert. I was finding this very hard to cope with. Were we about to lose another of our precious chidren? Not this time. After two weeks of serious sickness, God again touched Joseph and healed him. He is now a happy five-year-old, bubbling with life and vitality and attending preschool in his neat navy and white uniform.

I have no way of knowing just what the future holds for Joseph, but I praise God for sparing this miracle boy so many times and believe that he will surely be around for some time.

Although I could write an entire book on the children God has placed in our hands, Chipo is another very special case. She was born of an incestuous relationship and has cerebral palsy. When she came to us she could not walk, talk, or even sit up by herself.

We loved Chipo from the start and have worked with her and prayed for her until, today, she is running, playing and even beginning to talk. She may not be what many would call a "normal child," but she is making remarkable progress. She lifts her little hands to praise the Lord and realizes that it is because of Jesus that she came to know what it means to be loved.

When Joy arrived at the home from Kanyemba, the brutal murder of her mother had so filled her young life with sorrow that it seemed she would never have peace. As the years passed, however, her new name, Joy, became the hallmark of her life. Thirteen years later, she is in college preparing for a career in hotel management. There have been some struggles, but God has been faithful to her, and she, as our eldest African daughter, has made us very proud.

One day we got a call from a hospital asking us to care for a boy whose mother had died of AIDS. Lesley and I went to investigate.

The narrow hospital ward was crammed with cots, each containing a tiny, vulnerable baby with a tenuous hold on life. It was a depressing, impersonal and alien place smelling of dirty diapers and stale food.

As I looked into these cots I realized that the eyes of each baby were lifeless, dull and vacant. No smile brought light and life to their faces. They had been fed and changed, but they were lying there somehow conscious that something was missing from their lives. There was no one to hold them, to cuddle them or to play with them.

In those days, there were still serious questions about the consequences of too much contact with AIDS. So, they were being cared for physically, but they were being starved of love. It was a terrible thing to see.

I stopped by one cot, noticing that the little girl who occupied it had casts on both her feet. I learned that she had been in a children's home, but they had sent her back because of her club feet. Her name was Christine.

Christine lay very still, looking up at me with eyes

filled with utter hopelessness and dejection. I felt com-
pelled to reach down and pick her up in my arms. As I
held her and talked to her, the expression on her face
changed. A beautiful smile transformed a miserable in-
fant into a radiant child. Unable to hold back the tears, I
prayed: "Jesus, please send someone to love this little
girl."

I laid Christine down in her cot, watching the sparkle
fade until, eventually, the light went out in her eyes. She
lay there intuitively aware that she was unwanted.
Hopes of being held forever in warm loving arms had
been dashed once again. We walked out of the hospital
and got into my car. Resting my head on the steering
wheel, I sobbed and sobbed.

"God, please help those babies," I prayed. "Please
send someone to rescue them. I don't have anything left
to give. We already have the children's home and so
many other areas of ministry. I have no more energy.
There is nothing that I can do. But I plead with You to
do something, Lord."

We returned to Montgomery Heights, but thoughts
of Christine and the other neglected babies I had seen
remained uppermost in my mind prompting me to keep
praying for them. One day God said to me: "You do
something." I should have realized that when God put
that burden on my heart it was because He expected me
to do somehting about it. Peter, the little boy we had
gone to see that day, died, but God had used the visit to
expose to us the plight of those babies and to give us
His compassion for them.

At first there seemed no obvious way to help them,
but God had a plan, as always, and He chose to reveal
to us in a very unconventional way.

CHAPTER THIRTY-ONE

FIRE AND EXPANSION

One day, when lunch had finished and there was the usual clatter of plates and the hubbub of voices in the dining room, I looked out the window and saw smoke billowing up from the direction of the garbage pit. We didn't normally light fires there during dry season, so I rushed outside to see what was happening. To my horror, the tall elephant grass was ablaze.

I rushed back inside to raise the alarm. We would have to act swiftly to keep the fire away from the buildings. Quickly we organized ourselves and the older children to fight the flames which kept rearing up like scarlet monsters and advancing relentlessly to devour the dried grass at an alarming rate.

Buckets of water carried by the smaller children were hurled at the fire. Wet sacks were used to beat the grass, and trenches were speedily dug to divert the flames. With aching arms, and faces streaked with soot, we battled, shouting instructions above the crackling and roaring of this unleashed power that was threatening our lives. Eventually, the raging fire subsided, having burnt out its energy — and ours — in a furious rampage across our lands.

Later, when we had caught our breath, we walked across the blackened and still smouldering fields, with wisps of grey smoke periodically spiralling up to the vivid blue sky, like chiffon scarves twirled in a dance. Everything was peaceful now. We walked silently, each doubtless praising God for sparing us and our existing facilities.

Then suddenly we noticed something we had never seen before on the property and went to investigate. It seemed to be the foundation of a small building with walls about four feet high. Tall grass had hidden it from view before, but it was obvious that it was a strong and solid construction. We later learned that pigs had been reared at Montgomery at one time and that this building had been their pen.

As I looked at those foundations, pigs were not on my mind. Instead, with faith bubbling up in my heart, I could see a Baby Unit on this site, a home for those helpless, unloved AIDS babies for whom I had been praying.

It didn't look like much. Scorpions chased across the derelict shell of a building, and delicate flowers pushed up through cracks in the concrete. At the moment it was a worthless heap, but God was showing us the potential of this site as a haven of love for the defenseless and rejected. We had no idea where the money would come from and were not sure how we would set about the task, but we trusted God to show us what to do.

Many have asked me if we were not afraid to catch AIDS ourselves. No. We were prepared to use wisdom and to take precautionary measures, but we simply could not say no to those helpless children craving love. We could not allow scare-mongering, rumor-spreading and selfish concerns to prevent us from expressing the love of God to them.

From that day on, Jean Webster went to the site of the pigpen every morning to pray. She was not frightened off by the scorpions, baboon spiders and other assorted creatures. Day by day she cried to God to bring this vision to reality. And eventually, the building was begun.

Step by step, each obstacle was overcome and the walls went up and the roof went on. The interior was decorated with beautiful teddy-bear murals, painted on the walls by Louise, a short-term worker. Curtains, cots and toys were all provided in wonderful ways, and blankets, diapers and baby clothes began to fill the shelves of the storeroom. Finally, one day the water supply was hooked up, and the Baby Unit at Montgomery was ready to open its doors. It was August of 1995.

We had seen our first babies some weeks before in a hospital in the town of Marondera. They were twins who had spent the first seven months of their lives sharing a cot in a hospital ward. Chipo (a different Chipo, a common name meaning "gift") was sucking her thumb and did not seem very responsive, but Rutendo looked up at us, with those all too familiar vacant eyes, and stretched out her little arms. We picked up both babies and played with them and, before long, the loving touch of another human being ignited smiles that transformed their faces. When we returned them to their cot, they began to cry. It was hard to leave them that day, but we were soon back to take them to their new home.

The twins came to us on a Wednesday. They looked so cute in their yellow dresses. It caused my mind to travel back twenty-five years to the day I had received my first set of twins. That had also been on a Wednesday, and Gerrilynn had worn a yellow dress. My heart felt like it would burst with gratitude to God. All my tears of sorrow seemed to have brought forth a harvest of twins.

Actually, when we went to receive the twins, we came away with three babies. An agent of the social welfare system had asked us to take Nyasha too. He had AIDS and TB. His mother had died and the relatives who took him in had neglected him. He was soon back in the hospital suffering from malnutrition. His emaciated body was a pitiful sight, and on the long journey home in the car he maintained a haunting, pitiful cry like a wounded animal.

Now there are fourteen babies in the unit. Some are HIV positive, while others are sick with tuberculosis. Where a dilapidated pigpen once existed, there now stands a house ringing with the cries and laughter of contented babies, a house of love created by God Himself.

One of my greatest joys in serving God at Montgomery is that our twin daughters, Cheryl and Gerrilynn, have been working alongside us in loving and caring for the children. One day Cheryl and I sat in the social welfare office scanning a long list of names. The department was closing down a children's home because there had been neglect and abuse, and they still had about fifteen children to place. "How many can you take?" the social welfare lady asked anxiously.

My heart was heavy. We had already taken in five newly abandoned children that week, and we were running out of space. Montgomery was bursting at the seams.

Cheryl, still scanning the list, suddenly announced,

Fire and Expansion

"Look, Mom, twins! Scott and Erek are five years old, and Stella and Steven are three and a half." She paused and gave me a knowing look.

What could I say? "Well, we definitely have to take the twins," I replied. "There is no way we can leave here without them."

I praise God for the compassion He has given my daughters. They are such a blessing. If I had been able to have children in the normal way all those years ago, then I would have missed out on so much. I would not have been involved in the lives of Matthew, Cheryl and Gerrilynn, and I might not have taken on Montgomery Heights. God knows exactly what He is doing, and His plan is perfect.

What riches God has given us! The house we live in and the car we drive belong to the mission, and we have none of the status symbols used to measure success in the eyes of men, but we have riches beyond comprehension. The children who bear the name "Rozell," and other children in India, Africa and many other parts of the world are all part of the family God has given us. The years of childless torment are only a vague remembrance, as my arms overflow with children who call me Mother.

CHAPTER THIRTY-TWO

WHY ME, LORD?

Why me, Lord? I have asked Him the question so many times, and the only answer I ever get is because He loves me. The most capable people in the world and the least capable stand equal before Him. All that matters is His love and our response to that love.

What we become in God has absolutely nothing to do with human qualification and everything to do with His grace. Without the redeeming work of Christ in our hearts we are nothing, and can achieve nothing. With Him, nothing is impossible to us. The choice is ours to make.

The future does not depend on our past. We can choose the ways of God, or we can choose to go our own ways, whatever our past may have been. Being rich or poor, educated or ignorant, advantaged or disadvantaged, has nothing to do with it. God's love changes everything and opens every door to *whosoever will*.

God took the broken pieces of the life of the frightened little girl I was and made somebody of me. He called me by name and gave me a special work to do for Him. Although the hurts and scars from the past were not discarded easily, and sometimes the going was tough, yet deep in my heart, I have always known that God loved me, whatever else happened.

Today, God is calling many to serve Him. He is calling those who have considered themselves useless failures and who cannot believe that God would ever use them to fulfil His purposes. He is calling those who feel they have absolutely no qualifications and can recite a list of personal facts which they are sure will count them out. He is taking ordinary reeds and making them mighty by His power.

A lovely old chorus goes like this:

Something beautiful; something good,
All my confusion, He understood.
All I had to offer Him was brokenness and strife,
But He made something beautiful of my life.

What are the qualifications God places on those who will serve Him? Not education, not the right social background, not material prosperity, not image, not physical appearance, not any of the other factors that preoccupy human beings as they select candidates for prominent positions. The truth is that when God puts His hand on us and chooses us for His work, only He knows what He is about to do and how He is about to do it. We must only trust Him.

I believe very much in the value of education and I personally hold several degrees, but our educational tools cannot give us an anointing from God and are no substitute for His touch on our lives. The only way to get a job done in the Kingdom of God is to recognize that we are nothing and that He is everything.

When Jerry and I were teaching in Bible college in

America, we were disappointed to see that the students often didn't have the proper motivation. At one point, Jerry was led to take down all his degrees from the wall of his office and put them in a box. As the students came into the room over the next few weeks, many of them commented on the gaps on the walls. We told them that the real purpose of their time at the college was not obtaining a paper certificate of some kind, although that was important; it was to receive a vision from the Lord Jesus Christ and to be equipped by Him for service in the Kingdom.

God also does not choose us because we have an unblemished track record. His calling is not reserved for those who have remained totally faithful to Him since the first day of their conversion. We all make mistakes, and some of them may be serious, but making a mistake does not disqualify us from being chosen for a special task. If we turn to God in repentance and faith, we will discover that He is a God of forgiveness and restoration.

I love this old poem:

THE WEAVER

My life is but a weaving
Between my Lord and me.
I cannot choose the colours;
He worketh steadily.
Oftimes He weaveth sorrow,
And I, in foolish pride
Forget He sees the upper,
And I, the underside.
Not 'til the loom is silent
and the shuttles cease to fly,
shall God unroll the canvas

Why Me, Lord?

and explain the reason why.
The dark threads are as needful
in the Weaver's skilful hand
As the threads of gold and silver
In the pattern He has planned.
– Author unknown

Often God's plans are vastly different from mine. His thoughts are not like ours. As the Scriptures declare:

For my thoughts are not your thoughts, neither are your ways my ways, saith the Lord.   Isaiah 55:8

We make plans, hoping to turn our dreams into reality, but those plans are not necessarily the purposes of God for us. He has said:

Ye have not chosen me, but I have chosen you, and ordained you, that ye should go and bring forth fruit, and that your fruit should remain.   John 15:16

I have sometimes tried to engineer circumstances to bring about God's purposes, but this has proved to be sheer folly. To listen to Him and obey as each step is revealed has proven to be the only way forward. Don't be afraid to make a commitment to God today. Tell Him that you will follow where He leads you, whatever the cost.

An art professor asked his class to paint a picture depicting peace. The students produced flamboyant sunsets, country garden walls cascading with colorful flowers, calm seascapes and a whole range of other peaceful scenes.

A Reed In His Right Hand

As the professor paused before the work of one student, he looked confused. Vicious waves pounded on jagged rocks and the sky was dark and threatening. Trees, bent double by a violent wind, seemed to be sweeping the ground. "Son, I don't believe you understand this assignment," he said. "You were supposed to be painting a picture expressing your view of peace."

"Sir, can you see the little bird?" the student asked.

The professor leaned forward and looked more closely at the painting. On a limb of the tree, swaying and bending in the storm, a small bird was perched, somehow retaining its balance in all the upheaval. The professor could see that although the bird was battered by the brutality of the elements, it was still singing.

"Sir, that little bird is at peace," the student said triumphantly.

A bird singing in a storm. A reed held securely in God's right hand. Serving God is never easy, but He has promised us that His strength will shine through our human weakness, bringing glory to Him. This is the heritage of the children of God who are prepared to serve Him wholeheartedly.

Won't you be *"A Reed In His right Hand?"*

Notes

Notes

Notes

Notes

Notes

Notes

Notes

Notes